23.2.4.13

Different but the Same

Persons of the African-American and Caucasian Persuasion

my observations

Phillip J. Weathersby, III

iUniverse

DIFFERENT BUT THE SAME
PERSONS OF THE AFRICAN-AMERICAN
AND CAUCASIAN PERSUASION

iUniverse books may be ordered through booksellers or by contacting:

iUniverse
1663 Liberty Drive
Bloomington, IN 47403
www.iuniverse.com
1-800-Authors (1-800-288-4677)

Because of the dynamic nature of the Internet, any web addresses or
links contained in this book may have changed since publication and
may no longer be valid. The views expressed in this work are solely those
of the author and do not necessarily reflect the views of the publisher,
and the publisher hereby disclaims any responsibility for them.

Any people depicted in stock imagery provided by Thinkstock are models,
and such images are being used for illustrative purposes only.
Certain stock imagery © Thinkstock.

ISBN: 978-1-4917-7413-7 (sc)
ISBN: 978-1-4917-2646-4 (e)

Print information available on the last page.

iUniverse rev. date: 10/16/2017

Acknowledgment

I would like to thank two of the most influential persons in my life for their support, encouragement, wisdom, and love. I speak of my beautiful wife, Carol, and my adorable daughter, Morgan. Carol, my best friend, confidant, and love of my life has endured several years of me compiling all of the observations resulting from my travel and numerous interviews with people of both subject persuasions. I would like to thank her for believing in me and her consistent motivation when periodically business circumstances dictated otherwise. Her wisdom, clairvoyance, and fortitude played an intricate part in structuring the development of selected chapters in this book. As my best friend, I trusted her unwavering faith, interest, and motivation in inspiriting me to write this book with the absence of any reservations.

My daughter, Morgan, through her youthful insight and discernment, availed me of a unique perspective. Her enthusiasm was an absolute joy. I am so grateful for her encouragement and inspiration. My daughter has a propensity for acknowledging the uniqueness in people. In writing this book, I consulted with her on many occasions for her concurrence of observations in social settings of the subject included herein. For her patience and for my own frequent requests for social consultation, I thank her.

Quotes

"I believe Phillip has written a provocative, intensely engaging, and unprecedented compilation of observations unique to the two-dimensional medium but quite familiar and vivid to the human experience."

-Robert M. Greenville, Ph.D.
Charlotte, North Carolina

"Phillip's observations are undeniably witty, brilliantly composed, and frighteningly true."

-Arthur Smith,
Orlando, Florida

"Word on the streets is that people will read it, think it, see it, and perhaps experience it. Now that is powerful."

Kelly Anne Mosely
Arlington, Texas

"Phillip's book encourages motivations of forward thinking; to dismiss the veracity in his collection is pure fear and subconscious denial; one can be significantly enriched by experiences of other ethnic groups."

-Kathy L. Ingram, Ph.D.
Seattle, Washington

"Phillip J. Weathersby, III writing may project that he is mentally estranged and socially challenged, but in actuality, he is on point as he ingeniously depicts our mentally estranged behaviors and social challenges.

-Kevin A. Collier,
Birmingham, Alabama

"Phillip's book will jolt the fixed mind set into potential acceptance of truth."

-Ivan Willis
Trenton, New Jersey

Contents

Preface

Before you begin reading my interviewees 630 entries, allow me to share with you that I unavoidably experienced countless hours deliberating the "acceptable" description of both ethnicities as Blacks vs African-Americans and Whites vs Caucasian Americans. Subsequently, I elected to use African-American Persuasion and Caucasian American Persuasion because I am partial to the etymological flair. Political correctness was not an influence. I also would like to draw your attention to the word "most" which is used throughout my book. During my many interviews "most" was defined as "the majority" of interviewees who voiced their perspective on all subjects in my book. Now having said that, I implore your indulgence to assimilate the contents of my manuscript.

History has shown us how race relations between persons of the African-American Persuasion and the Caucasian Persuasion have eroded and also have perpetuated and elevated dissension, fear, hatred, and violence. Racial differences and ethnic tensions have been embedded in this country arguably for nearly four-hundred years. It rears its ugly head in business, politics, education, communities, and many other facets of life. In this contemporary society, the illusion and silent sentiments of what one deems good race relations has once again proven to be politically and socially unhealthy. Some sense of veracity has to present itself in order to thwart the expansion and deterioration of the racial divide.

Occupants of this society, especially those of the African-American and Caucasian Persuasions are keenly mindful of vitriolic positions and political maneuvering that deepen the ills of this country and shred the audacity of hope for a better society. Unity is vital. It is our responsibility to mitigate politically charged racial negativity, pessimism, and self-victimization which enables one group to blame another group for all their failures. We have come to know this hypothetical racial experimental off-Broadway play, lightheartedly as "Us Against Them" and it has entirely run its course. It is old and predictable. New writers should engage with what will perhaps change the racial trajectory and help launch positive dialogue and encourage acceptance.

The play, "Us Against Them" should provide multiple topics and settings that highlight a collection of unique characteristics of each ethnic group. Those unique features can conceivably show serious and lighthearted dissimilarities. The development of dissimilarities from each ethnic group may generate notable idiosyncrasies that can be described as "nothing positive, nothing negative" but "it is what it is." Although each ethnic group has generous differences (pros and cons), the individuals in each cluster are human beings all of whom were created by a higher power (GOD) who is the absolute essence of love, life, acceptance, peace, and unparalleled embodiment of compassion.

Each ethnic group is unique, but each primarily wants the same out of life, i.e., love, prosperity, freedom, peace, and happiness. So, one that has a sense of understanding and acceptance of their differences can say, we are "different but the same." The majority of the interviewees expressed that neither ethnic group has the rights to determine what another group should or should not have. Who are we to judge and have such disdain for another group we didn't create? Yes, there are self-appointed "gods" and "goddesses" that choose to be unhappy, angry, and who have a profound contempt for another group regardless of circumstances they believed encouraged such a temperament. The interviewees and my experience have afforded us to believe, individuals of the African-American and Caucasian Persuasions that continuously speak or act on depravity against each other; in most instances, these individuals have an extreme disliked of themselves; that are fearful, spiritually bankrupt, and fragile. However, there is optimism, and we trust that ethnic observations call for acceptances, open communications, corrective attitudes, and non-judgmental allowances or tolerance in all departments in life.

I have written this book to share with you some of the different idiosyncrasies of African-Americans and Caucasian Americans that I have observed for the past thirty years. It is my hope that this collection generated by over 3,200 interviews and observance for the past ten years from Seattle to Orlando and Los Angeles to New York will perhaps precipitate a better tolerance of ethnic behavior. I, also with great enthusiasm, wish to encourage readers to engage in dialogue about these observations, and learn that my view of activities and multiple conversations with African-Americans and Caucasians may prove to be accurate.

Friends, colleagues, coworkers, and family members forewarned me that the interviewees, my observations, and interpretations may cause many readers to become irate, perturbed, or basically "pissed off." However, the same group of acquaintances and family members has expressed that they also believe readers will find these observations funny, interesting, engaging, clever, and "on the money."

I have always questioned physical gestures and the behavior of African-Americans and Caucasians when confined or when positioned in similar environments. Why do their actions and reactions differ significantly? Yes, there have been multiple historical, philosophical, psychological, and neurological studies conducted and theories formulated as to why African-Americans and Caucasians do what they do in similar settings. Although many studies and theories have been conducted, the average person may loathe the concept of dissecting endless arguments. Additionally, the interviewees shared with me that they believe the average person has no interest in these findings only because the research was designed around limited behavior and environments. This book is not a study, per se. It is simply the interviewees and my honest observation of the actions and reactions which I have personally witnessed most African-Americans and Caucasians display in given circumstances.

By understanding the common behavior of most African-Americans and Caucasians in multiple environments, one may conclude that this is surprisingly the norm. It is evident that most African-Americans and Caucasians are reared in primarily different and separate sub-cultures. Take for example, most African-Americans are reared and educated in predominantly African-American communities and are exposed to their global levels of importance and contributions to society. Similarly, most Caucasian Americans are raised and educated in predominantly Caucasian American communities and are exposed to their global levels of importance and contributions to society as well. Some argue that these communities should remain separate while others articulate the need to unite them. Nonetheless, while both arguments have merit, this book merely depicts my attention to noticeable dissimilarities in various degrees between persons of the African-American Persuasion and individuals of the Caucasian Persuasion in the United States, particularly in the Western, Midwestern, Southern, Southeast, and East Coast regions of the United States.

I have chosen not to reveal my ethnicity because I only want to invoke curiosity from the reader, although my ethnicity will inevitably be made known. I want to introduce the comments of interviewees and my impartial observances that delineate particular distinctions between African-Americans and Caucasian Americans (the subjects) and not about my ethnicity. I have been advised that a small group of readers and perhaps people, who only hear about the book without reading it, will spew out the vicious and depraved commentary in an attempt to dismiss or refute content and what I have observed and what over 3,200 individuals have shared with me as well. People with such driven disposition will always exist. Haters will always be haters, and hurt people have an acute propensity to harm others employing or creating vile and unconstructive remarks. I have also been forewarned because of the subject matters to anticipate potential creative mendacities and other means of discharging negativity. Nevertheless, I welcome all readers.

Additionally, this book is not written to heighten or highlight a particular ethnic group or provoke hatred between persons of the African-American and Caucasian Persuasions. My questions generated from many years of interviews and observations are not personal, although some readers will take them as such. My ultimate objective for each reader is to provoke thought, facilitate tolerance, change, and share what each ethnic group is silently expressing more often than one would envision and finally, to encourage understanding.

Chapter 1
Business Settings

Business Setting

The business chapter questions and captures the mindset of business owners of the African-American and Caucasian Persuasions in contemporary business operations. These series of questions were generated and compiled by numerous interviewees who expressed their uncensored views on each other's persuasion. This chapter is the result of my observations and valued input by persons of the African-American and Caucasian Persuasion experiences, practices, and desired reasoning behind familiar and unfamiliar ethnic perceptions and business motivations. Their approach to business solutions is uniquely special and complex, although each persuasion has the same aspirations and focus, including establishing private businesses that sustain marketability, meeting particular demands or needs, and subsequently, yielding reasonable expectations of profitability. Society's social elements dictate the winners and losers. Both persuasions are not totally defined by their business triumphs or losses, but by their moral fortitude, compassion for their patrons, and responsibility as citizens.

Business is defined as the activity of purchasing and selling commodities, products, or services. These practices of entrepreneurship have existed for centuries and produced generations of wealth. The idea that it has allowed persons of the African-American Persuasion to do business simply is relatively novel in comparison to the generations of business longevity of Persons of the Caucasian Persuasion have enjoyed. Thus, business methods, approaches, opportunity outlooks, and ideologies of doing business vary substantially between both persuasions, but their interests and motivations for prosperity for their families remain the same.

African-American and Caucasian interviewees in various municipalities and communities throughout the country have graciously shared interesting perspectives on the basic approach of establishing a business and the unique perceptions and challenges one may experience. These perspectives and challenges range from securing capital, target marketing, community acceptance, family and investors support, the impact of money circulation in their community, and a myriad of detailed observations. Surprisingly, in-depth knowledge of business principles and management theories did not necessarily advance either persuasion's business opportunities. Relationships and potential financial business sustainability were the pivotal elements that allowed them to remain in business and heighten their future business projections. Those elements weighed significantly in capturing the ways and means that elevated their business. However, in these exceptional years of equal business opportunities, interviewees departed communications that unveiled business practices of the early twentieth century which thwarted one ethnic group from enjoying the business entrepreneurial "level playing field."

Unabashedly, the Caucasian business owners infer that the social order has provided them the "best of both worlds." They expound on the phrase by stating that African-Americans openly support their businesses with little to no reservations. Some even decline to do business with other African-American businesses in their communities that offer the same products or services. African-Americans discount their distance traveled outside of their communities to support Caucasians businesses. Clarifying a step further, Caucasians support each other's businesses. African-Americans support their businesses overwhelmingly as well which hence the quote, "best of both worlds." Financial resources are secured by individuals and institutions that are managed and operated by persons that look like them. Caucasian interviewees also shared that other elements associated with operating a successful business such as suppliers, distribution, advertisement/marketing, accounting, capital investment, banking, legislation, and recruitment services which often are rendered by persons that look like themselves. One interesting factor is that their clientele is diverse and in some scenarios, all of their clientele is of the African-American Persuasion. Usually, when there is diversity, Caucasian Americans have a firm hold on the economic and business impact in what is otherwise a majority African-American community. Thus, African-American and Caucasian money circulates at least ten times in the Caucasian business communities which in turn, increases business ownership and builds generational businesses and wealth. Conversely, African-American money circulates at a maximum of one time in African-American communities.

The African-American business owners conveyed a different perspective in conducting business affairs. They revealed "the best of both world" mentality simply did not exist in their business developments and practices. African-American business owners said that in most cases, the African-American does not support African-American businesses regardless of competitive services and prices. They shared that those African-Americans who do support their community businesses often complain about prices being too high, poor service, employees attitudes, that the facility is not the most aesthetically pleasing or offers an inviting environment, and their businesses are unwilling to significantly reduce their prices. Unexpectedly, the same African-Americans who complain barely utter their discontent openly in Caucasian business establishments. African-American business owners rarely recall occurrences where Caucasians bypass other Caucasian owned businesses within their communities to travel any considerable distance to purchase or secure services from African-American owned business where both ethnic groups offer the same products or services. The African-American business owner interviewees expressed their exceedingly challenging and disappointing experiences in securing real estate, suppliers, distribution outlets, advertisement/marketing, accounting, capital investment, banking, staffing, legal, and favorable legislation to help with business start-ups and sustainability. The African-American business owners interviewed hardly ever recall vying for the above elements and resources where the services are rendered by persons that look like them. In the majority of instances, services are rendered by a person of the Caucasian Persuasion, are believed in most cases, to be either not as supportive or unwilling to operate in their best interest.

Statistics outline the fact that all Caucasian and African-American businesses are not entirely successful, nor are they of absolute failures. Business challenges are inevitable, but one ethnic sector believes hard work is the sole factor to surviving in business. Another ethnic sector believes hard work is important, but history, individual, and group mindsets are not aligned with their potential, hopes, work ethics, and dedication to a thriving business. This chapter highlights some of their experiences and beliefs. These represent the majority of interviewees and my observations.

Business Observations / Differences

The Mindset Of Doing Business

1. *Business -Why is it that* when a private or public entity requests a firm of the Caucasian Persuasion to encourage 15% to 20% minority participation in business opportunities and construction projects, protests and expressions of resentment immediately begin to emerge? The immediate defense disposition displays an uncooperative and greedy frame of mind, especially when it is determined that the person of the Caucasian Persuasion is unequivocally guaranteed at least 80% to 85% participation and the majority of the profit.

2. *Business-Why is it that* most interviewees expressed that successful business firms of the Caucasian Persuasion rarely, if ever, volunteer to establish business relationships with a successful person or firm of the African-American Persuasion? An attempt towards this effort is usually initiated with reluctance, and only when a private or public entity for which they want to do business requests or requires said arrangement.

3. *Business-Why is it that* most interviewees expressed that businesspersons or firms of the Caucasian Persuasion consistently equate the adjective "qualified" as being synonymous with businesspersons or firms of the African-American Persuasion? In most scenarios, when persons or firms of the Caucasian Persuasion address the aforementioned business opportunities, "qualifications" and "African-Americans" are joined at the hip. Rarely does one identify Caucasian owned businesses as "qualified" before contractual negotiations. Does the absence of such description of Caucasians depict what is dubbed as a given in both African-American and Caucasian communities?

4. ***Business-Why is it that*** most interviewees expressed that businesspersons or firms of the Caucasian Persuasion, when given a business opportunity, vehemently express that they earned the privilege to do business, worked hard to be selected to render services, and paid their dues for the opportunity to do business? However, when businesspersons or firms of the African-American Persuasion are given a business opportunity, it is frequently expressed that said persons or firms received a handout, are free-loading, or got work only because they were of the African-American Persuasion. Seldom do they earn any business opportunities of significant monetary value and many persons of the Caucasian Persuasion believe that is how it should be. Is this mentally embedded in thought?

5. ***Business-Why is it that*** most interviewees expressed that some businesspersons or firms of the African-American Persuasion find it highly impossible to succeed in the business arena (especially in a city where African-Americans make up 50% or more of the population) with the absence of a person or firm of the Caucasian Persuasion as a major partner with at least 35% to 60% interest in the business arrangement? However, most Caucasian owned businesses can and have succeeded without any participation from or with African-American involvement in the same business arena.

6. ***Business-Why is it that*** most interviewees expressed that businesspersons or firms of the African-American Persuasion seem to work much harder to sustain and maintain a solvent business? Nevertheless, the businessperson or firm of the Caucasian Persuasion defines the African-American businessperson's actions and disposition as listless, out of their league, and characterize the reasoning behind their minute growth as simply their lackadaisical work ethics.

7. ***Business-Why is it that*** most interviewees expressed that businesspersons or firms of the Caucasian Persuasion that express their commitment to associate or enter into joint ventures/consult with persons or firms of the African-American Persuasion consistently conclude that their fees are always excessive? To avoid further potential business associations, the persons or firms of the Caucasian Persuasion quickly revert to their Caucasian associates with the absence of conducting reasonable negotiations with the persons or firms of the African-American Persuasion. Do they want to do business or is it the old proverbial smoke screen of facilitating business appeasement?

8. ***Business-Why is it that*** most interviewees expressed that businesspersons or firms of the African-American Persuasion that associate with other business persons or firms of the African-American Persuasion do considerably less business than in their business associations with a person or firm of the Caucasian Persuasion with a similar business approach and objective?

9. ***Business-Why is it that*** most interviewees expressed that when the majority of businesspersons or firms of the African-American Persuasion establish a strong, competitive, successful, and prosperous business, it is immediately assumed by African-Americans that said businesspersons or firms are secretly controlled or owned by persons of the Caucasian Persuasion?

10. ***Business-Why is it that*** most interviewees expressed that in the African-American community, the dollar circulates approximately one time for business services and consuming opportunities, whereas, in the Caucasian Persuasion community, the dollar circulates at least nine to ten times in business transactions? Additionally, most interviewees believe

that African-Americans' spending or purchasing power is without doubt admirable, but they find it perplexing as to why African-Americans do not support each other in order to grow their communities and create wealth.

11. ***Business-Why is it that*** in most major cities in the United States where African-Americans represent at least 50% to 65% of the population, African-Americans own less than 5% of all real estate property and building structures in the Central Business District?

12. ***Business-Why is it that*** most interviewees expressed that male persons of the Caucasian Persuasion commonly pat an African-American male on the back at the beginning or conclusion of a business meeting and shake the hand of other male persons of the Caucasian Persuasion? How often does one see an African-American male pat a Caucasian male on the back during an introductory greeting?

13. ***Business-Why is it that*** when most male persons of the Caucasian Persuasion, who have reaped the benefits of opportunities given to them by their hard work, decide to purchase a new luxury car or home; their peers and most persons of the African-American Persuasion that observe the new purchase rarely question their financial ability to afford such luxuries or the financial source by which they acquired such wealth? However, if the same scenarios were applied to an African-American male with equal or greater opportunities, persons of both the Caucasian and African-American Persuasions would question and investigate their purchases and financial resources exhaustively.

14. ***Business-Why is it that*** some persons of the African-American Persuasion, in primarily Southern states, who have Caucasian business colleagues that make up approximately 60% to 75%

of the workforce have a tendency to speak with an unusual but pronounced southern nasal dialect? This southern nasal, dialect (or drawl, if you will), is most noticeable in the pronunciation of the following words or grouping: Thank you, door, fire, for, here, hear, their, over there, sit, seat, chair, day, do, that, and they, just to name a few. However, the persons of the Caucasian Persuasion do not verbally communicate in the same southern dialect of persons of the African-American Persuasion.

15. ***Business-Why is it that*** most interviewees expressed that female businesspersons of the Caucasian Persuasion exert every effort to maintain short hair styles, whereas most business females of the African-American Persuasion tend to pursue longer hair styles even to the point of adding hair extensions? Are they going through this exercise to secure approval from other women or men? Is the average businessperson really fixated on hair length when it is quite evident that it is not natural or original?

16. ***Business-Why is it that*** most interviewees expressed that persons of the Caucasian Persuasion rarely have or voluntarily establish office appointments with physicians of the African-American Persuasion regardless of their expertise or specialty?

17. ***Business-Why is it that*** most interviewees expressed that persons of the African-American Persuasion visit physicians who are not of the same persuasion when the percentage of African-Americans that graduate medical and dental schools has increased substantially in the past fifteen to twenty years and have practices ready for services?

18. ***Business-Why is it that*** in most professional or technically advanced academic settings, persons of the Caucasian Persuasion infrequently acknowledge or credit the contributions of persons of the African-American Persuasion in the fields of

architecture and engineering when it is historically recorded that said persons made countless contributions?

19. ***Business-Why is it that*** most interviewees expressed that young male and female persons of the African-American Persuasion who work as employees in fast food, specialty, and clothing establishments display little respect for the average customer, especially customers that happen to be of the same persuasion? On frequent occasions the employee lacks prompt service, does not enthusiastically or timely acknowledge the costumer's presence, and rarely offers a simple thank you at the completion of any product purchase. Often the employees discuss openly to each other their personal matters, and when doing so, profane language is commonly used with no consideration or desire to extend an apology to the customer. Why does management condone such extreme lack of service professionalism?

20. ***Business-Why is it that*** on any major thoroughfare or vehicular circulation system that spans one to two miles in any U.S. city and has a majority African-American population of approximately 50% to 65%, African-Americans have less than 5% of commercial, retail property, and building ownership?

21. ***Business-Why is it that*** most interviewees expressed that persons of the African-American Persuasion verbally suggest and expect unreasonable discounts and credits from other African-American business owners during the purchase of any product, but rarely expect or verbally express the same interest with Caucasian business owners?

22. ***Business-Why is it that*** most interviewees expressed that persons of the African-American Persuasion are more suspicious of other persons of the African-American Persuasion who have amassed financial wealth, but cheerfully applaud persons of the Caucasian Persuasion who have achieved the same?

23. ***Business-Why is it that*** most interviewees expressed that persons of the Caucasian Persuasion are more often accused and even convicted of extortion, embezzlement, fraud, and money laundering crimes perpetuated by greed more so than persons of the African-American Persuasion?

24. ***Business-Why is it that*** the overwhelming majority of picture frames that are for purchase in any store and any community are donned with sample photos of persons of the Caucasian Persuasion but are rarely donned with persons of the African-American Persuasion?

25. ***Business-Why is it that*** persons of the African-American Persuasion are the first to be killed in drama or action movies when the lead person is of the Caucasian Persuasion?

26. ***Business-Why is it that*** some male persons of the Caucasian Persuasion publicly unleash their bitterness and title themselves as "The Angry White Male" or express, "We need to take back our country" when they hold most corporate executive positions, and control judicial and legislative branches of government, financial institutions, construction industry, the stock exchange institution, primary, secondary and higher education institutions, medical, legal, gaming, entertainment, motion picture industry; and are CEOs, COOs, CFOs and board members of most Fortune 500 corporations?

27. ***Business-Why is it that*** some male and female persons of the Caucasian Persuasion in the workplace bring their own lunches or "brown bag-it" more often than persons of the African-American Persuasion? It has been determined that this effort of bringing a lunch daily is a means of saving money. What do most persons of the African-American Persuasion do to reduce daily lunch expenditures?

28. ***Business-Why is it that*** some male persons of the Caucasian Persuasion applaud and foster the philosophy that "Nothing Is Too Much" for male persons of the African-American Persuasion? This philosophy is subconsciously exercised when financial matters are in questioned. A large number of African-Americans believe persons of the Caucasian Persuasion would rather that they have nothing than allow them to experience a financially level playing field. Some African-Americans also believe that persons of the Caucasian Persuasion benefit from actions which ultimately keep them powerless and broke but toss out a bone now and then to diminish potential public and political backlash.

29. ***Business-Why is it that*** when persons of the Caucasian Persuasion who are responsible for various office business tasks become overwhelmed and frustrated, their immediate supervisor extends some sense of sympathy and authorizes a mental daybreak, but when the same situation occurs with workers of the African-American Persuasion, their supervisors deem them as inexperienced or incompetent?

30. ***Business-Why is it that*** male and female persons of the African-American Persuasion who have historically been considered economically disenfranchised and understand the assumed effortlessness with which a single person of the Caucasian Persuasion can gain wealth, have failed to pool resources to capitalize on new economic ventures? Perhaps this is tied to the lingering argument that it takes five to ten African-Americans to do what one Caucasian can do regarding raising capital. Are these doors purposely closed to African-Americans?

31. ***Business-Why is it that*** persons of the Caucasian Persuasion rarely consider persons of the African-American Persuasion in serving as their realtor, architect, attorney, physician, accountant, financial adviser, or any other professional service,

whereas most persons of the African-American Persuasion, when pursuing the same group of professionals, mostly pursue and select persons of the Caucasian Persuasion?

32. ***Business-Why is it that*** persons of the Caucasian Persuasion who enter the field of engineering, (i.e., aerospace, biological, computer, chemical, electrical, mechanical, etc.) have a greater desire and ambition to establish their own companies, while most persons of the African-American Persuasion are less desirous to have their own business and are more inclined and untroubled to work for someone else until retirement? Is this highly technical industry reluctant to accept business ownerships or advance significant opportunities for persons of the African-American Persuasion?

33. ***Business-Why is it that*** most interviewees expressed that persons of the Caucasian Persuasion rarely establish direct eye contact with persons of the African-American Persuasion when addressing a mixed audience of both Caucasians and African-Americans? Eye contact remains constantly fixed on persons of the Caucasian Persuasion but quickly wanes from persons of the African-American Persuasion.

Unnecessary And Avoidable Energy

34. ***Business-Why is it that*** most interviewees expressed that male and female persons of the Caucasian Persuasion have a tendency to ignore the presence of male and female persons of the African-American Persuasion during large business functions? Their presence is deemed tokenism, and their level of importance is regarded as insignificant.

35. ***Business-Why is it that*** most interviewees expressed that persons of the Caucasian Persuasion who are in business rarely have to provide their financial statements, office

physical location, number of full-time employees, tax return information, payroll information, listing of liquid assets, liability or professional errors and omissions insurance, ownership, stock options, distribution of shares, etc. to qualify to render services for public or private entities? Conversely, persons of the African-American Persuasion who are certified in Minority Business Enterprise (MBE), local, or state programs have to provide all of the above and more just to be considered to do business, but are not guaranteed any business opportunities.

36. ***Business-Why is it that*** most interviewees articulated that persons of the African-American Persuasion painlessly facilitate the financial success of persons of the Caucasian Persuasion but begrudge the concept or find it immeasurably difficult to champion the financial success of persons of the African-Americans Persuasion? Most persons of the African-American Persuasion work hard and do not express any economic discomfort to see that persons of the Caucasian Persuasion can afford to place their offspring in private educational academies and relocate to suburban American.

37. ***Business-Why is it that*** most interviewees expressed that persons of the Caucasian Persuasion painlessly facilitate the financial success of other persons of the Caucasian Persuasion but try inconspicuously, and often anonymously, to prevent the financial success of persons of the African-American Persuasion? Most persons of the Caucasian Persuasion do not have any interest or could not care less about the financial success of any person of the African-American Persuasion.

38. ***Business-Why is it that*** most interviewees expressed that persons of the Caucasian Persuasion criticize persons of the African-American Persuasion for poor personal financial management, debt, and bankruptcy that range from $15K to $30K, but when persons of the Caucasian Persuasion

experience the same circumstances at greater amounts, i.e., $50K top $150K, they are rarely criticized for poor financial management? However, persons of the Caucasian Persuasion can land back on their feet and start anew more often with greater ease and less difficulty than those of the African-American Persuasion.

39. ***Business-Why is it that*** most interviewees expressed that persons of the Caucasian Persuasion criticize persons of the African-American for poor personal business management, debt and bankruptcy that range from $50K to $500K, but when persons of the Caucasian Persuasion experience the same circumstance at greater amounts i.e., $150K to $5 million, they are rarely criticized for poor financial management? However, persons of the Caucasian Persuasion can land back on their feet and start anew more frequently and with greater ease or less difficulty than persons of the African-American Persuasion. African-Americans are permanently labeled, ruined for life, and are not encouraged to have successful rebounds.

40. ***Business-Why is it that*** most interviewees expressed that a large number of persons of the African-American Persuasion do not collectively support with enthusiasm financial institutions, such as banks, credit unions, or insurance companies that are owned and operated by African-Americans, especially when most African-Americans clearly understand the insurmountable odds that have been historically stacked against them?

41. ***Business-Why is it that*** most interviewees expressed that persons of the Caucasian Persuasion rarely use the services of, or support financial institutions such as banks, credit unions, or insurance companies that are owned and operated by African-Americans, especially when most Caucasians clearly understand the insurmountable odds that have been historically stacked against them? They know that they have endured endless acts of cruelty, discouragement, and other deterrence in their struggle.

42. ***Business-Why is it that*** most interviewees believe persons of the Caucasian Persuasion are the prime decision makers of most realtor associations that establish and determine the property value in all communities? Typically, the property value is greater in predominantly Caucasian middle-class neighborhoods, and property value is less in predominantly African-American middle-class neighborhoods of similar size, location, school district, aesthetics, and standards.

43. ***Business-Why is it that*** most interviewees believe persons of the Caucasian Persuasion are more often reluctant to do business voluntarily with persons of the African-American Persuasion, even if the latter are more educated, have been in business longer, and have been awarded by their business peers and the community as businessman or businesswoman of the year?

44. ***Business-Why is it that*** most interviewees believe persons of the Caucasian Persuasion fear and detest the concept or the mere utterance of persons of the African-American Persuasion experiencing an equal or level playing field when it comes to business opportunities?

45. ***Business-Why is it that*** when most male persons of the Caucasian Persuasion who are employed in high-level white collar jobs are suddenly relieved from their jobs, they are more likely to find employment quicker with equal or higher pay and status than male persons of the African American Persuasion?

46. ***Business-Why is it that*** most interviewees expressed that persons of the Caucasian Persuasion equate or compare "Gay Rights" to that of the African American's struggle to achieve

"Civil Rights?" These two depictions of rights are entirely dissimilar.

47. ***Business-Why is it that*** when African-Americans come up with clever ideas to improve the quality of life for all of society, they seem to be compelled to present it to persons of the Caucasian Persuasion in order to clench approval and to successfully secure finances and marketing? Conversely, Caucasians never feel compelled to secure approval, share an idea, or seek financial assistance from persons of the African-American Persuasion.

48. ***Business-Why is it that*** most interviewees believe that in most African-American communities, persons of any nationality are allowed to set up shop on corners with very little protest or resistance from African-Americans that reside within or outside of the community? Conversely, communities that are largely of the Caucasian Persuasion protest or resist such entrepreneurial outlets, although the same zoning laws apply in both communities.

49. ***Business-Why is it that*** the movie industry frequently depicts African-American females as overly emotional and permits African-American males to use invective language excessively to the point the viewer feels verbally assaulted?

50. ***Business-Why is it that*** most interviewees expressed that persons of the Caucasian Persuasion who have been indicted, prosecuted, and sentenced, serve no more than five years in federal prison for stealing (embezzling, defrauding, misappropriating) millions or billions of dollars from their employees or the public, while person of the African-American Persuasion will serve more than five years in local and state prisons for stealing less than $500.00 from a local grocery store?

51. ***Business-Why is it that*** in the twenty-first century, most persons of African-American and Caucasian Persuasions still find it difficult to accept any African-American serving as their immediate supervisor or boss regardless of their impressive level of intelligence, experience, or qualifications?

52. ***Business-Why is it that*** most male interviewees of the Caucasian Persuasion expressed that they frequently receive inner strength, moral, and financial support from their families and colleagues when initiating meaningful business ventures? On the contrary, male persons of the African-American Persuasion perhaps may elevate their inner-strength to forge ahead, but rarely receive any support from family members or others when initiating meaningful business ventures. Their reluctant support usually defines theirs business venture as risky.

53. ***Business-Why is it that*** most interviewees expressed that persons of the Caucasian and African-American Persuasions in corporate America who are in positions to hire personnel are more inclined to hire persons of the Caucasian Persuasion to replace an African-American who has been fired more often than persons of the African-American Persuasion, even if their credentials are extremely similar? Is their apprehension that the fired person represents the standard behavior or performance of all African-Americans, thus considering hiring another "qualified" African-American as too great a risk?

54. ***Business-Why is it that*** most interviewees expressed that persons of the Caucasian Persuasion who own businesses in predominantly African-American communities, and amass generational financial wealth from them, have to be asked to consider or encourage diversity in future business opportunities?

55. ***Business-Why is it that*** most interviewees expressed that persons of the Caucasian Persuasion consistently have reservations about the ability, qualifications, and performance of the leadership of persons of the African-American Persuasion in business transactions, even when they serve as subordinates?

56. ***Business-Why is it that*** nearly all interviewees expressed that most male and/or female persons of the Caucasian Persuasion in private or public meetings address male persons of the African-American Persuasion by their first names and address persons of the Caucasian Persuasion by their sir names, even if the male person of the African-American Persuasion is the senior co-worker, colleague, or senior personnel?

57. ***Business-Why is it that*** nearly all interviewees of the Caucasian Persuasion expressed that some lyrics in some African-American rap music are so excessively perverted and incredibly demeaning to the African-American community that some listeners have felt they needed to dash for a bath or to the nearest vomitorium, and repent to God for their indulgence?

58. ***Business-Why is it that*** most African-American believe large recording labels primarily owned by persons of the Caucasian Persuasion turn a blind eye to African-Americans rap artists' rude behavior against other African-Americans and condone their crass, degrading, abhorrent obscenities toward each other and market primarily in the African-American community? Why do African-American male rap artists and the African-American community allow this demoralizing behavior to become common practice for the sake of the dollar?

59. ***Business-Why is it that*** when persons of the Caucasian Persuasion, who have owned construction, engineering, computer, marketing, or financial services businesses for twenty years or more, and have cornered the market in

providing a particular service, then lose a bid to an African-American business, they will ruthlessly attempt to shut them down, discredit them, and often launch an investigation to determine their eligibility, fairness, and qualifications? The action as mentioned earlier is rarely conducted to the extent of that of an African-American business when a Caucasian business wins a bid over another Caucasian business.

60. ***Business-Why is it that*** nearly all interviewees expressed that most "blue collar" African-Americans will work for a Caucasian-owned business for minimum wage all day, every day with under breath complaints, but will work less, demand more money, and become quite vocal regarding complaints while working for an African-American-owned business?

61. ***Business-Why is it that*** nearly all interviewees expressed that most "blue collar" persons of the African-American Persuasion will work harder, longer, and for less pay at a minimum wage for entrepreneurs of the Caucasian Persuasion, but do not work as hard, or as long, and certainly not for less pay at a minimum wage for African-American entrepreneurs? In fact, some interviewees believed that increased pay would be the primary issue every day on the job and said group would begin to disparage the owner publicly.

62. ***Business-Why is it that*** most interviewees articulate that male persons of the Caucasian Persuasion regard their spouse as revered beings, but the minute they enter the business world and become successful, their pleasant depictions of them are removed and they are then degraded and often deemed as evil bitches?

63. ***Business-Why is it that*** most interviewees expressed that persons of the Caucasian Persuasion who are in the market to purchase a new home of $300K or more are provided more

creative options, consistently and overwhelmingly outpacing African-Americans in qualifying for secure financing? Realtors, mortgage firms, and bankers divulge options to persons of the Caucasian Persuasion that are far from traditional, i.e., financing a home with two different mortgages or an interest only mortgage at a lower interest rate than most persons of the African-American Persuasion. With low-interest rates, one can pursue "House Flipping" and clear $50K to $100K easily to eventually purchase a home debt free.

64. *Business-Why is it that* most interviewees expressed that persons of the African-American Persuasion who are in business and have a unique and impressive product or service are encouraged by both Caucasians and African-Americans to consider the ethnicity of the messenger (business community is more receptive to a Caucasian) when marketing and vying for opportunities?

65. *Business-Why is it that* most interviewees expressed that persons of the Caucasian Persuasion do not believe persons of the African-American Persuasion will generate interest or maintain ratings on today's popular reality series? They also do not have any interest in characterizing or extending constructive depictions of persons of the African-American Persuasion.

66. *Business-Why is it that* nearly all interviewees expressed that persons of the African-American Persuasion in the corporate environment equate hard work as performing a given task with physical labor? Conversely, most persons of the Caucasian Persuasion equate hard work in the same corporate environment as finding or directing others to perform the task for them and reaping the accolades as a job well done.

67. ***Business-Why is it that*** most interviewees expressed that persons of the African-American Persuasion have a tendency to feel guilty about unique and highly competitive job opportunities that they have secured? Do most subconsciously believe that they are preventing a person of the Caucasian Persuasion from the same or equal opportunity?

68. ***Business-Why is it that*** most interviewees expressed that persons of the African-American Persuasion are very reserved in networking and less gregarious when working a room at a business conference that is predominantly occupied by persons of the Caucasian Persuasion?

Generations Of The Wrath But Business As Usual

69. ***Business-Why is it that*** most interviewees expressed that persons of the Caucasian Persuasion, especially Caucasian females, find it difficult to accept the fact that an African-American male can serve as a self-employed professional marketing or business consultant? Their first instinct is that he is unemployed. Secondly, they ask: "why he is not working for someone?" They may also assume his unemployment is perhaps caused by him not being a team player. Finally, they ask how he is doing this?

70. ***Business-Why is it that*** most interviewees expressed that entrepreneurs of the African-American Persuasion do not plan aggressively for retirement, (i.e., standard IRAs, Roth IRAs, mutual funds, savings, etc.)?

71. ***Business-Why is it that*** nearly all interviewees expressed that persons of the African-American Persuasion who do business fairly are consistently bilked by most persons of the Caucasian Persuasion when they are in positions of power and influence? Subtle actions of inequity against persons

of the African-American Persuasion go undetected, (i.e., pay increase, annual bonuses, exposure to other business associates, introductions to personal business associates "I know a friend who knows a friend," advice on investment options and opportunities, etc.).

72. ***Business-Why is it that*** nearly all interviewees expressed that persons of the African-American Persuasion unmistakably understand the viewpoint that "Power Equates Financial Ascension," or "Power Equates Wealth," or "Wealth Equates Power" as practiced more often by persons of the Caucasian Persuasion, but rarely experience it for themselves?

73. ***Business-Why is it that*** nearly all interviewees expressed that male persons of the Caucasian Persuasion when being introduced by a standard business handshake for the first time to a male person of the African-American Persuasion, intuitively return their hand to its original position after slapping the thigh with an open palm?

74. ***Business-Why is it that*** most interviewees expressed that persons of the Caucasian Persuasion who handle money in their line of business frequently return change from $1, $5, $10 etc., to persons of the African-American Persuasion by placing it on the counter in lieu of in their hands, even when the African-American initially provided and placed the appropriate funding in their hands?

75. ***Business-Why is it that*** in most motion pictures, the African-American male is portrayed as deviant, poverty stricken, and less than professional?

76. ***Business-Why is it that*** complaints of persons of the Caucasian and African-American Persuasions about the attitude and customer service of African-Americans in any business

venue are usually venomous to the point of demeaning or discrediting them regardless of the minutest problem they may have experienced? In most cases, complaints and criticisms are not as vicious when services are rendered by persons of the Caucasian Persuasion.

77. ***Business-Why is it that*** most interviewees expressed that male persons of the African-American Persuasion believe with very little reservations, that the majority of male persons of the Caucasian Persuasion in similar employment earn approximately 20% or greater in annual income? Most African-American males question the merit of such financial increase when the same position is held, and the same level of work is rendered.

78. ***Business-Why is it that*** most interviewees expressed that persons of the Caucasian Persuasion downplay, dispel, belittle, and in some circumstances, detest hard working ethics of persons of the African-American Persuasion? Why is it that those that begrudge their work ethics are adamant about any new business opportunities or economic advances that are awarded to persons of the African-American Persuasion and judge their moments as handouts in lieu of good work ethics that facilitated positive change?

79. ***Business-Why is it that*** most interviewees expressed that persons of the African-American Persuasion who serve the public, (i.e., city council, county, official, school boards, etc.) exercise unusual restraint or have reservations when openly recommending African-Americans for professional services? Conversely, persons of the Caucasian Persuasion rarely exercise restraint when recommending Caucasian Americans for professional services. In fact, they are rather boastful about their experience and expertise.

80. ***Business-Why is it that*** most interviewees expressed that persons of the African-American Persuasion consistently lag financially behind persons of the Caucasian Persuasion in most levels of business, (i.e., engineering, architecture, law, accounting, real estate development, food and retail franchises, automotive dealerships, sports team ownership, etc.) even with a larger workforce and more experience?

81. ***Business-Why is it that*** most interviewees expressed that persons of the Caucasian Persuasion, who have risen to an admirable financial status primarily through an inheritance, from "who you know" business opportunities, from the backs of the poor, or, swindled the uneducated and disadvantaged, force the opinion that most African-Americans should execute self-reliance and refrain from depending on assistance from others?

82. ***Business-Why is it that*** most interviewees expressed that person's actions of the Caucasian Persuasion strongly suggest that persons of the African-American Persuasion still do not have or will never possess the intellect or business maturity to render any professional service successfully? The interviewees further expressed that most persons of the Caucasian Persuasion actions convey the message that most African-Americans should be content with an employee status in lieu of being the employer.

83. ***Business-Why is it that*** the African-American male is the least, and more than likely, the last to be considered for employment as a professional highly paid white-collar worker in comparison to the Caucasian male, Caucasian female, or African-American female? It is common practice to employ the above individuals in the following order: Caucasian male, Caucasian female, an African-American female, and reluctantly the African-American male.

84. ***Business-Why is it that*** most interviewees expressed that most African-American females and males view the actions of most Fortune 500 corporations and homegrown local companies as ones that are intentionally encouraged to limit the employment elevation of African-Americans to top positions? Most African-Americans who have vied for promotions have experienced endless reasons for not advancing as rapidly as persons of the Caucasian Persuasion regardless of their intellect, experiences, productivity, creativity, work ethics, team player disposition, responsibility, accountability history, etc.

85. ***Business-Why is it that*** most interviewees expressed that persons of the African-American Persuasion give in to the ideology that most persons of the Caucasian Persuasion consciously and subconsciously depict their ethnicity as one that is graced with favor? However, most African-Americans unquestionably believe favor is no respecter of persons. Nevertheless, they consistently choose not to empower themselves by not granting other African-Americans business opportunities when they are in positions to do so.

86. ***Business-Why is it that*** nearly all interviewees expressed that most male persons of both the African-American and Caucasian Persuasions are more inclined to buy business products, supplies, professional services, and mostly anything a Caucasian female has to offer? The African-American female has found it more difficult to make a sale in comparison to the Caucasian female. However, the African-American male has found it increasingly more difficult to just secure an audience, let alone make a sale.

87. ***Business-Why is it that*** nearly all interviewees expressed that most persons of the Caucasian Persuasion consistently believe that when persons of the African-American Persuasion are provided an opportunity to work, said employment subsequently denies an employment opportunity for a person of the Caucasian Persuasion?

88. ***Business-Why is it that*** nearly all interviewees expressed that most persons of the African-American Persuasion believe that most persons of the Caucasian Persuasion get better interest rates when purchasing homes or simply taking out a personal or commercial loan? Most African-Americans also believe that most Caucasians receive at least half of a point, up to two points less in interest rates on the above financial matters. They accept as true that Caucasians receive more, longer, and better opportunities, which equate to more money, fewer defaults, and more to pass down to future generations.

89. ***Business-Why is it that*** nearly all interviewees expressed that most persons of the African-American Persuasion are not intricately engaged in Dow Jones Index, NASDAQ Composite Index, S & P 500, American Stock Exchange, Russell 2000 Index, Wilshire 5000 Index, etc., at a significant or notable level?

90. ***Business-Why is it that*** nearly all interviewees expressed that persons of the African-American Persuasion believe that if they were publicized recipients of corporate bonuses ($20M to $50M) from Merrell Lynch, Bear & Stern, AIG, Citigroup, and other national investment corporations, federal regulatory policies limiting such rewards would have been implemented twenty years ago? They believe that persons of the Caucasian Persuasion would be fiercely outraged of the above bonus more so than present day sentiments

91. ***Business-Why is it that*** nearly all interviewees expressed that persons of the African-American Persuasion expect other persons of the African-American Persuasion who have amassed wealth to contribute to every church function, fish fry, school

fundraiser, etc., but seldom solicit other ethnic business owners in their communities who have profited substantially from their patronage?

92. ***Business-Why is it that*** only two or three American persons of the African-American Persuasion in the United States are among Forbes' list of American 400 billionaires since 2004, which equates to .005% representation? Where are the African-American billionaires who are male athletes, professional sports franchise owners, movie and music artists, clothing designers, international industrialists, real estate moguls, retail business owners, shipping tycoons, Silicon Valley entrepreneurs, cable media entertaining moguls, and health care family-owned corporations? What is missing? Is the playing field level or do African-Americans have the talent, education, intellect, drive, exposure, business savvy, work ethic, and most definitely investors and investment capital?

93. ***Business-Why is it that*** nearly all interviewees expressed that persons of the African-American Persuasion who happen to be in business can quickly recite at least five persons of the Caucasian Persuasion who are being trained or groomed to take over family businesses? Whereas, most persons of the Caucasian Persuasion find it difficult to recite quickly at least five African-Americans being trained or groomed to take over family businesses.

94. ***Business-Why is it that*** nearly all interviewees expressed that most persons of the African-American Persuasion who hold key positions (purchasing agent, facilities management, physical plant, contract administration, etc.) in city, county, parish, state, and federal government find it difficult to defend an African-American firm or company when or if misinformation occurs, or when they make an error that is of little significance? Instead, most individuals in the above list will allow persons of the

Caucasian Persuasion to belittle, discredit, and ostracize them, eventually resulting in their dismissal or lost opportunity to secure any work. However, Caucasians will defend a Caucasian firm that experiences the same miscommunication or error and will encourage continued services, or grant a second, and third opportunity to render various services.

95. ***Business-Why is it that*** most interviewees expressed persons of the African-American and Caucasian Persuasion work hard to find or create any professional associations or state registration infractions against an African-American male professional, (i.e., architect, engineer, attorney, teacher, physician, etc.) to simply discredit or penalized them? In most cases, the association responds aggressively initiating investigations based on one colleague's allegations but do not thoroughly consider the plaintiff's suspicious ulterior motive. Once the investigation is announced, and the result is proven to be false, the plaintiff remains anonymous, and the regulatory body moves on, but the damage has already been done.

96. ***Business-Why is it that*** a large number of persons of the African-American and Caucasian Persuasion rarely experience the pleasant and frequent sight of exclusively three to four African-American males or females having a business lunch on consistent basis?

97. ***Business-Why is it that*** most salespersons in all facets and levels of the construction supply business, pharmaceutical, first, second, and third tier automotive supply industry, furniture, clothing, environmental systems, medical, literary, and other industries are 99.9% of the Caucasian Persuasion?

98. ***Business-Why is it that*** most interviewees expressed persons of the Caucasian Persuasion are astoundingly reluctant to do business with persons of the African-American Persuasion,

especially African-American males regardless of their multiple years of entrepreneurial success?

99. ***Business-Why is it that*** most interviewees expressed persons of the Caucasian Persuasion have systematically limited the business opportunities of African-Americans by delaying or denying property acquisition, financing, mentoring sponsorship, legislation initiative, and state and federal grant administration and, through voluminous and endless application and registration requirements, to be identified as a diverse entity, while remaining poised and eager to proclaim that they have not been in business long enough to understand the dynamic and intricate business deals?

100. ***Business-Why is it that*** a large number of male persons of the Caucasian Persuasion are consciously fearful and detest the concept of an African-American male having equal footing in securing governmental Department of Defense contracts, state and local major construction contracts, and top positions in private major architectural and engineering design services, petroleum, banking, securities, insurance, and communications?

101. ***Business-Why is it that*** nearly all interviewees expressed that most persons of the African-American Persuasion believe approximately ten persons of the African-American Persuasion are equivalent to three persons of the Caucasian Persuasion when raising and establishing capital for developing business ventures?

102. ***Business-Why is it that*** nearly all interviewees expressed that most persons of the Caucasian Persuasion have successfully controlled persons of the African-American Persuasion from employment, financing, purchasing power, real estate, education, business ownership, and all levels of advanced

business opportunities? As a result, unemployment in the African-American community is in the double digits in comparison to Caucasian American. There is an extremely small population of African-American wealth managers, multi-million dollar real estate brokers, and business owners.

103. ***Business-Why is it that*** most interviewees expressed that persons of the African-American Persuasion believe that most persons of Caucasian Persuasion have a sustained and deliberate motivation to cap particularly African-American males from advancing in professional services?

104. ***Business-Why is it that*** most interviewees expressed that persons of the African-American Persuasion believe that most persons of Caucasian Persuasion motivation in life is "money?" Most African-Americans also believe the motivation mentioned above confirms their belief of the sustained and deliberate fervor of persons of the Caucasian Persuasion to limit particularly African-American males from advancing in the financial arena.

105. ***Business-Why is it that*** most interviewees expressed that persons of the Caucasian Persuasion are more inclined to define their worthiness and placement in lucrative jobs or prestigious positions primarily on their due diligence, effort, and hard work, whereas, most persons of the Caucasian Persuasion defined the placement of persons of the African-American in lucrative jobs or prestigious positions primarily as a result of "Affirmative Action?" Frequent quotes expressed by persons of the Caucasian Persuasion upon the hiring of an African-American include: "He or she only got that position because he or she is black," "Well, you know we had to hire one but he or she won't stay long;" "They are taking over all our jobs" and "If one more is hired, I'm finding me another place to work."

106. *Business-Why is it that* nearly all interviewees expressed that most persons of the African-American Persuasion are disproportionally envious of other persons of the African-American Persuasion when one experiences a sizable business opportunity or a large financial windfall? Additionally, African-American recipients of windfalls are inundated with donation requests from every church, school, and non-profit community organization.

107. *Business-Why is it that* nearly all interviewees expressed that most persons of the Caucasian Persuasion are unhindered in securing ownership of real estate or business opportunities by any person of the African-American Persuasion? They believe African-Americans may have educational, and business attributes that are extraordinary but they are not in significant leadership decision-making positions to approve or deny anyone anything.

108. *Business-Why is it that* nearly all interviewees expressed that most Historically Black Colleges and Universities are leery and afraid to secure sizable business services of African-Americans? Businesspersons of the African-American Persuasion are mostly denied business opportunities from primarily the CFO Office, Facilities Management or Athletic Director's Office. Conversely, most business opportunities at said colleges and universities are granted to persons of the Caucasian Persuasion through the CFO Office, Facilities Management, or Department of Athletic

109. *Business-Why is it that* nearly all interviewees expressed that most Predominantly White Institutions are leery and afraid to secure sizable business services of African-Americans? Businesspersons of the African-American Persuasion are mostly denied business opportunities from primarily the CFO Office, Facilities Management or Athletic Director's Office.

Conversely, most business opportunities at said colleges and universities are granted to persons of the Caucasian Persuasion through the CFO Office, Facilities Management, or Department of Athletics.

110. ***Business-Why is it that*** nearly all interviewees expressed that most business owners of the African-American Persuasion rarely hold the deed to the commercial property location for which they have been doing business for the past 25 years?

111. ***Business-Why is it that*** the median net worth of most persons of the Caucasian Persuasion has increased substantially between 2005 and 2015 approximately 18 to 20 times that of persons of the African-American Persuasion?

112. ***Business-Why is it that*** the unemployment rate for persons of the African-American Persuasion is approximately 7.5% as compared to 3.7% for persons of the Caucasian Persuasion, whereas the U. S population of persons of the Caucasian Persuasion (63%) is approximately 4.8 times greater than the population of persons of the African-American Persuasion (approximately 13.1%)? Should not the larger population have a larger percentage of unemployment?

113. ***Business-Why is it that*** most interviewees expressed that most male persons of the Caucasian Persuasion in the financial arena who have been given employment opportunities from other male persons of the Caucasian Persuasion systematically denied male persons of the African-American Persuasion employment opportunities, access to financing, purchasing power, real-estate, education, and business entrepreneurship at multiple levels, but falsely and solely hold responsible the repeated denials of the male persons of the African-American Persuasion?

114. ***Business-Why is it that*** most interviewees expressed that most male persons of the Caucasian Persuasion consciously or subconsciously deem most persons of the African-American Persuasion as problems? Regardless of the Caucasian's socio-economic status, (i.e., dirt poor or exceptionally wealthy) they believe that persons of the African-American Persuasion are not worthy by one iota of any financial growth if it exceeds their financial status level by a dime.

115. ***Business-Why is it that*** most interviewees expressed that most male persons of the Caucasian Persuasion deem themselves as entitled to life employment and business opportunities over any person of the African-American Persuasion, regardless of their level of education or business savvy?

116. ***Business-Why is it that*** most interviewees of the African-American Persuasion expressed that most male persons of the African American Persuasion who have or attempted to establish a business or secure ownership of sizeable property, believe that the rounds of unnecessary business challenges they consistently experience are reasonable facsimiles of the "1638 Maryland Doctrine of Exclusion?"

117. ***Business-Why is it that*** most interviewees expressed that most persons of the African American Persuasion accept as true that persons of the Caucasian Persuasion deem themselves as "entitled" to any inkling of prosperity regardless of their level of education, experience, or qualifications? Their expression of thought is "after 400 years; they still want to take from us our hard earned money." Why is it that most persons of the Caucasian Persuasion accept as true that persons of the African American Persuasion are not entitled to any forms of "entitlement?" Their expression of thought is that "they are lazy and all they want is another handout."

118. ***Business-Why is it that*** most interviewees expressed that most persons of the African American Persuasion believe that the political and business machines mainly governed by persons of the Caucasian Persuasion cleverly and purposely diluted the foundation and potential power of an African-American Minority Business Enterprise (MBE) by including every ethnic and political group that exists? African-American MBE believes every ethnic and political group has solely and significantly benefited from their torturous decades of struggle with the absence of any legislation prohibiting their participation in capitalism.

119. ***Business-Why is it that*** most interviewees expressed that business persons or firms of the Caucasian Persuasion believe that African-Americans will allow any tyrannical (demeaning, humiliating or ignoring) treatment from persons of the Caucasian Persuasion with the absence of immediate and direct action to address or correct said treatment?

120. ***Business-Why is it that*** most interviewees of both African-American and Caucasian Persuasions believe that most large professional businesses that vie for sizable municipal, school districts, and higher education professional services are heavy participants in the "pay to play or good ole boy" politics, especially those firms that are frequent contract recipients? They also believe by design most African-American firms cannot afford to "pay to play" and are not in the "good ole boy" alliance. Thus, most conclude that without the absolute presence or association with a Caucasian firm, the African-American firm will not be awarded said work even if the public entity's leadership is 100% of the African-American Persuasion. Moreover, the interviewers believe that African-American firms must have an association with Caucasian firms as prime or equal participation to make it official or justifiable.

121. ***Business-Why is it that*** most of the African-American and Caucasian interviewees question why African-Americans have not decided to forgo their 400 years of wretched desire to be accepted by persons and communities of the Caucasian Persuasion and develop housing, create business (finance centers, food markets, clothing, technological enterprises, communication outlets, etc.), vigorously, re-educate, build communities, and demonstrate the power of their numbers? The interviewees also asked why African-Americans do not substantially curtail spending in other communities and aggressively increase business transactions within their communities? Some interviewees believe if African-Americans accept the challenge to building their communities and that if all-compassing transformation is realized, physical destruction by persons of the Caucasian Persuasion, city and state governing bodies will exert every effort to thwart and block implementation, governing policies will change prohibiting such actions, and the list goes on. Moreover, nearly all interviewees also suppose the majority of African-Americans believe persons of the Caucasian Persuasion loathe their existence and desire to play on equal grounds. However, when African-Americans choose to have their own, persons of the Caucasian persuasion are predictably motivated to put a stop to their drive and ambition. Most African-Americans are of the sentiment "we are damned if we do and damned if we don't" and Caucasians "fear, envy, and hatred are immeasurably deep."

122. **Business-Why is it that** most male African-American interviewees believe avarice, self-importance, and chicanery were characteristics of a large amount of male businesspersons of the Caucasian Persuasion that led to the near total ruination of the U.S. financial market? They ask why no one was charged, indicted, and prosecuted. They also believe that lack of judicial action and fairness is evident most Caucasian Americans of wealth can do mostly anything they desire and escape prosecution.

Chapter 2
Politics

Politics

The political climate in today's society is viewed as toxic by interviewees (both African-Americans and Caucasians Americans). Two words, fair and comprise, once stood for hope and progress that perhaps could be potentially beneficial to all persons of any persuasion but today they do not exist. The hard line and unwavering stance on various issues have stymied growth, derailed freedom, and destroyed the concept of common sense. Recent presidential elections have heightened radicalism and provided excuses for ethnic groups to amplify their disdain for other ethnic groups. It seems as if spewing vile and demeaning inferences towards other ethnic groups is commonplace. Sadly, some political neophytes incite such crass behavior among their constituents, mainly less informed ones, in hopes that it may secure votes and victory over their opponents. Politics may be defined as the art or practice of influencing people and government policy. There are reasonably other definitions but the actions of politics today should include the total exclusion of interest of one particular ethnic group and the total inclusion of interest of another ethnic group. This growing movement has reduced common judgment for the good of all ethnic groups to immeasurable lows. This movement is prevailing and "in your face."

The majority of African-Americans interviewees expressed their frustration of treatment by most Caucasian Americans and their growing political fronts that are designed to further discount and exclude them from any level of prosperity, power, or control, outside of sports and entertainment. The interviewees also shared their continuing and increased irritation of Caucasian Americans marginalizing their experiences in multiple life scenarios. One, in particular, is the simple treatment by law enforcement regardless of their intellect, income status, residence location, and accompanied association. Another irritation African-American have is employment, especially among African American males. Unemployment of African-Americans is in double digits and has been parked there for over five years. African-Americans believe that if the Caucasian American males' unemployment exceeds 10 percent, it will become a national crisis. Local, state, and federal legislation would filter through with expedience. While the African American males unemployment is approximately thirteen percent and national coverage is minimal, their plea for work opportunities is largely ignored, and the political culture/machine welcomes other distractions to use as a means to not open employment opportunities for them, and begin to express vile comments as: "they need to get off their lazy asses and find a job; they don't want to work; and they want government to take care of them." Most African American interviewees also believe unemployment percentages are at least 50 percent higher than Caucasian Americans at every educational level.

The majority of Caucasian American interviewees expressed their stretched and breaking point of intolerance of African-Americans, complaining about unemployment, being misrepresented as a group, demand for higher wages, lack of caring teachers, better schools, access to higher education, building the nation, and their "innocent" and horrific experiences with law enforcement. Continued conversation on race places them in an awkward position which causes an extraction of guilt and humility. They believe that as individuals, they have not experienced the benefits of entitlements, nor have they caused the high rate of unemployment among African-Americans and the personal wealth gap between African-American and Caucasian Americans. Caucasian Americans contend as an individual of a larger ethnic group, their advances in politics, education, business, professional services industry, corporate America, and other dominantly held positions in public and private sectors were the results of hard work, determination, and a level playing field of opportunities for both African-Americans and Caucasian Americans. The perception is that African-Americans choose not to work as hard and that they lack the determination and want special treatment.

Underscored in this chapter are the political movement impacts, interests, and views of persons of the African-American and Caucasian Persuasions. Their interest and views are quite revealing. Questions have been asked as to why policy initiatives across the country have shifted to devalue and weaken voting strength, and discount contributions made by one particular group and exercise relentless efforts to derail any wealth generating opportunities and power shifts. Their action communicates the need to expand the continuous influence of other groups.

The African-American's political interests vary greatly from those of the Caucasian Persuasion. The African-American interviewees expressed that their interests are education, true representation of African-American interests, not grouped with other "minorities," and placed into one minority block: unemployment, jobs, fair wages, and private and public business opportunities. Caucasian American interviewees expressed that their interests are education, removal of the government regulation arms in the first and second amendments, freedom to do whatever they want to do, religious freedom, control, wealth, and power. Both ethnicities vie for peace, a strong and safe family unit, job sustainability, and prosperity.

This chapter is a compilation of other inquiries and views that African-Americans and Caucasians seek to understand each other. This collection of inquiries is the true curious interest and experience of both ethnic groups. Some questions may seem favorable to each group, and some may not seem so favorable, but that is exactly the purpose of this book: to call attention to the perception of varied dissimilarity between African-Americans and Caucasian Americans. These represent the majority of interviewees and the majority of my observations.

Political Observations / Differences

The Gripping Reality

1. *Politics-Why is it that* the majority of interviewees expressed that most adults of the African-American Persuasion are perceived, grouped, and labeled as moderates, liberals, or ultra liberals by most persons of both the Caucasian and African-American Persuasions? However, they are innately, behaviorally, economically, and politically postured as survivors (one that continues to function or prosper in spite of opposition, hardship or setbacks) and minutely conservative.

2. *Politics-Why is it that* most state legislators of the African-American Persuasion may be categorized when entering office as having middle-class status and rise to seniority ranking eight to ten years later, but leave with the absence of effective business arrangements or substantial wealth as compared to the average state legislator of the Caucasian Persuasion with identical status?

3. *Politics-Why is it that* most interviewees expressed that most males of the Caucasian Persuasion who are in the lower-middle-class socioeconomically are more vocal and driven to encourage military aggression against any foreign force even when said acts are to the detriment of the aggressor's force?

4. *Politics-Why is it that* most interviewees expressed that most males of the Caucasian Persuasion are more inclined to vote or encourage the passage of legislation that will minimize or eliminate economic growth, participation, percentages, and language that impact the well-being of disadvantaged male and female persons of the African-American Persuasion?

5. ***Politics-Why is it that*** most interviewees expressed that most females of the Caucasian Persuasion have unquestionably advanced and/or gained more significant financial advantages than any other ethnic group with the implementation of "Affirmative Action" legislation that encouraged or mandated ethnic opportunity programs? However, most Caucasian females' spouses consistently and vehemently oppose such programs when they attract African-Americans.

6. ***Politics-Why is it that*** a number of male freelance or employed journalists on local and national scenes, who happen to be of the African-American Persuasion, publicly and intensively ridicule, demean, and discredit other persons of the African-American Persuasion, especially when the subject matter is racism? Refutation of such civil injustice is paramount in their argument.

7. ***Politics-Why is it that*** nearly all interviewees expressed that persons of the Caucasian Persuasion are quick to define or label a person of the African-American Persuasion as their African-American ethnic voice, spokesperson, or leader, but fiercely rebuke any person of the Caucasian Persuasion to serve as their ethnic spokesperson or leader?

8. ***Politics-Why is it that*** nearly all interviewees expressed that most male and female persons of the African-American Persuasion who publicly denounce and defame other persons of the African-American Persuasion are quicker to sever professional relationships or friendships to satisfy or vie for likeability in the Caucasian Persuasion's political and inner social circles?

9. ***Politics-Why is it that*** nearly all interviewees expressed that most persons of the African-American Persuasion have moral reservations about U.S. military aggression, especially

unprovoked, preempted initiatives against forces of color, and particularly if they have small military capabilities?

10. ***Politics-Why is it that*** nearly all interviewees expressed that most persons of the Caucasian Persuasion vociferate that they know what is best for persons of the African-American Persuasion in any circumstance? They believe most persons of the African-American Persuasion do not know what is best for themselves because they lack cultural exposure, political savvy, financial empowerment, and advanced education. Most interviewees asked themselves, is the "deficiency" a result of deliberate and generational affirmative advancement of Caucasian Americans?

11. ***Politics-Why is it that*** nearly all interviewees expressed that most persons of the Caucasian Persuasion consistently label young male persons of the African-American Persuasion as violent, thugs, callous, demonic, and societal mass murderers? Conversely, most African-Americans believe history clearly interprets that young male persons of the Caucasian Persuasion have been and are more inclined to violence (mass murders) and have exterminated countlessly more non-Caucasians than persons of the African-American Persuasion.

12. ***Politics-Why is it that*** nearly all interviewees expressed that most persons of the African-American Persuasion were ignored, written off, and deemed unpatriotic by most persons of the Caucasian Persuasion when they questioned the original charge to enter war from the past United States President George W. Bush to remove Muslim groups such as JIHAD and AL-QAEDA leadership? Most African-Americans continue to question why the U.S. spent billions of dollars searching for "Weapons of Mass Destruction" to "Free IRAQ civilians from its evil Dictator-Saddam Hussein," and remove the threat of "Imminent Danger" during a time the United States economy

was severely in distress, especially in the African-American communities.

The Hold Of Power, Control, And Fear

13. ***Politics-Why is it that*** nearly all interviewees expressed that most male persons of the African-American Persuasion are not outraged by the alarming presumed statistics that show more young African-American males are in prison than in colleges and universities? Why hasn't the African-American political population or an aggressive and influential front emerged to reverse sustainably said statistics?

14. ***Politics-Why is it that*** nearly all interviewees expressed that most persons of the Caucasian Persuasion truly believe that persons of the African-American Persuasion will never be or become as patriotic as they are, even those who have served in the armed forces and are presently classified as veterans?

15. ***Politics-Why is it that*** most interviewees expressed that most persons of the Caucasian Persuasion view themselves as overseers or the preferred ones when it comes to human rights of other nations, whereas the majority of all ethnic groups observations historically and vividly illustrate contrary actions?

16. ***Politics-Why is it*** that most interviewees expressed that most male persons of the Caucasian Persuasion who have political leadership acquiesce and become engrossed in the methodological theory of thesis, antithesis, and synthesis when making racial slurs, belittling and demeaning persons of the African-American Persuasion, and then attempt to make amends with said group?

17. ***Politics-Why is it that*** most interviewees expressed that most persons of the African-American Persuasion questioned the possibility of a conspiracy with the past George W. Bush

Presidential administration and the oil production industry as a conceivable reason to enact the declaration of war in Iraq? They believed oil prices increased drastically for no reason, especially when the United States has ample oil reserves, but allowed the oil industry to secure exorbitant profits. They deem such act as pure greed without any regard to their needs or interests.

18. ***Politics-Why is it that*** most interviewees expressed that most male persons of the Caucasian Persuasion exude uncontrollable enthusiasm when the United States utters the concept of going to war with a force or country that is half as wealthy and powerful? But, the reactions of most male persons of the African-American Persuasion are more subdued; they believe in and endorse the "Exhaust All Options" approach before going to war.

19. ***Politics-Why is it that*** most interviewees expressed that most persons of the African-American Persuasion proudly express their respect and patriotism for the United States but are always reminded of the country's founding principles of greed, the pillaging approach of acquiring wealth, and depraved dehumanization tactics used to build this great nation? Most African-Americans believe amassing said wealth by law, especially from the backs of their ancestry via free labor, is a concept that cannot be easily dismissed?

20. ***Politics-Why is it that*** most interviewees expressed that most persons of the Caucasian Persuasion believe that persons of the African-American Persuasion should get over the fact that their ancestors were slaves (that was then and this is now) and moved on with life? Why should they have a collection of guilt even though current and past generations benefited greatly from the evils of slavery sanctioned by this great nation and its elected leadership?

21. ***Politics-Why is it that*** most interviewees expressed that persons of the African-American Persuasion who serve in some political capacity, either elected or appointed, are not pooling bright thinkers and human resources that can effectively address, as well as implement, proactive concepts that will drastically reduce the number of young African-American males being introduced to prison life?

22. ***Politics-Why is it that*** most interviewees expressed that most persons of the African-American Persuasion fail to understand the power of their vote? Their actions are consistent with the predictions of persons of the Caucasian Persuasion which is "No Show and No Vote," especially when "it ain't warm out and the sun ain't shining."

23. ***Politics-Why is it that*** most interviewees expressed that most persons of the Caucasian Persuasion understand and fear the power of the African-American vote? Is it because of the possibility that African-Americans' revelation of political power is synonymous with control? Why is it that most persons of the African-Americans Persuasion believe their voting right is always under attack?

24. ***Politics-Why is it that*** most weekly worship services that are attended predominantly by persons of the African-American Persuasion allow persons of the Caucasian Persuasion to address them on political issues, especially when they are seeking election or re-election? Nevertheless, rarely do weekly worship services that are attended predominantly by persons of the Caucasian Persuasion allow persons of the African-American Persuasion to address them on political issues. Are African-Americans allowed or do they ask to address congregations that are predominantly of the Caucasian Persuasion?

25. ***Politics-Why is it that*** most interviewees expressed that most African American legislators on the state and federal scenes represent mainly African-Americans and disenfranchised constituents, but rarely introduce legislation that specifically addresses their needs? How often do they represent the affluent and well informed?

26. ***Politics-Why is it that*** when a concept or bill is introduced to a committee by a respected and seasoned legislator who happens to be of the Caucasian Persuasion, legislative members have a tendency not to contest his or her integrity and to receive the proposed legislation more seriously? Conversely, when their Caucasian colleagues support a legislator who has the same senior status and happens to be of the African American Persuasion, both African American and Caucasian legislators do not receive the proposed legislation as seriously.

27. ***Politics-Why is it that*** most interviewees expressed that most persons of the African-American Persuasion have not taken advantage of economic opportunities by working hard to experience the level playing field which persons of the Caucasian Persuasion consistently express that exists? By obtaining a secondary education and graduating college with multiple degrees, it should enable them to secure the best-paying jobs and economic power. This empowerment should provide assured positions (prior to the election of the first African-American President Barak Obama) as a U.S. Senator, Speaker of the U.S. House of Representatives, the U.S. Attorney General; becoming governor of any state, major TV network chairman and lead news anchor, chairman of top country clubs in any state, president of Ivy League, SEC, and Big Ten colleges and universities, chairman of two of the top five Wall Street investment and financial institutions, chairman of one of the top three defense contractors, chairman of five of the top ten bonding and construction companies, owner of one of the top

three pharmaceutical companies, owner of at least $250 million worth of real estate in a central business district in any major U.S. city; awarded solely local, state, and federal design and construction contracts totaling $100 million dollars or more, and other top positions in corporate America. Will hard work, optimism, experience, keen business savvy, and talent catapult them to these levels of opportunities or is there something else missing? Society has consistently voiced that the attributes as mentioned above will guarantee anyone success, regardless of ethnicity. Why is it that most persons of the African-American Persuasion believe that the level playing field does not exist for them but exists only for the ethnic group of the Caucasian Persuasion who is in financial control and call the shots?

28. **Politics-*Why is it that*** most interviewees expressed that most persons of the African-American Persuasion between the ages of 18 to 25 seem to care less about the struggle African-Americans experienced to acquire simply the constitutional right to vote? Some do not "give a damn." Thus, their continued practice, lack of political participation not only belittles their historic struggle but also weakens their effort to secure voting power.

29. **Politics-*Why is it that*** most interviewees expressed that most persons of the African-American Persuasion believe doors of opportunity are consistently closed when it comes to filling state high-level governmental appointments regardless of the hard work and support afforded an elected political candidate? Persons of the Caucasian Persuasion frequently fill the most high-level department and cabinet positions in most governors administrations.

30. **Politics-*Why is it that*** most interviewees expressed that most persons of the African-American Persuasion believe that if and when an African-American holds an office of power (i.e.,

mayor, governor, U.S. Senate, Speaker of the U. S. House of Representatives, Chief of Staff, and President) one has to have extraordinary credentials exceeding those of most persons of the Caucasian Persuasion who have held said positions historically? Why is it that most African-Americans and Caucasians believe that when an African-American male holds any of the positions as mentioned earlier, the state of the city, state or union is in or vastly approaching economic ruins.

31. ***Politics-Why is it that*** most interviewees expressed that most persons of the Caucasian Persuasion of means are more inclined to give and unequivocally support millions of dollars of foreign humanitarian aid and the push for democracy in foreign countries, but detest the deliberation of assisting African-American and Caucasian homeless and poverty stricken families in their town or city who are in acute need?

32. ***Politics-Why is it that*** most interviewees expressed that a female person of the Caucasian Persuasion is usually and overwhelmingly more likely to become elected as governor of a state first with little education and political experience before a male person of the African-American Persuasion with substantial education and political experience?

33. ***Politics-Why is it that*** the national news networks rarely, if ever, request or invite professors of law from Historically Black Colleges and Universities to serve on political panels in order to converse and discuss current events? However, if and when said entities respond, it is usually a celebrated African-American candidate who is seeking political positions.

34. ***Politics-Why is it that*** African-Americans primarily are the only ethnic group that disseminate and divulge "problems" and "issue" to the world via television and radio broadcasting "problems" and "issues" that plague their communities?

Panels of noted African-American leaders discuss openly what problems exist, how they emerged, and how to correct them. However, the same issues remain paramount year after year. Discussions linger, and some matters worsen. Why is it that panel members always conclude in their debate that the lack of family values, parenting, self-respect, opportunities, and financial security are the culprits that permeate the community and stagnate progress? Do they unify and resolve any significant social or economic issues?

35. ***Politics-Why is it that*** most interviewees expressed that most persons of the African-American Persuasion equate "Black Power" as a united effort to improve equality, experience a level playing field, increase opportunities, expand their financial base, encourage community business participation, garner respect from the majority ethnic group, and improve business and personal respect for each other? But, most persons of the Caucasian Persuasion equate said phrase with militant demagoguery, violence against people of the Caucasian Persuasion, and demands for leadership positions (by any means necessary) in all business and political facets of society.

36. ***Politics-Why is it that*** most interviewees expressed that most persons of the Caucasian Persuasion equate "White Power" as a united front to force ethnic superiority, promote one's heritage, protect continuous ethnic political, financial, judicial and military control, and maintain the prerogative to engage in lawlessness at the determent of other ethnic groups? Persons of the African-American Persuasion equate said phrase as a means to conduct business and facilitate lawful ethnic disparities that were embodied in Jim Crow Laws before the Civil Rights Movement.

Depraved Intentions

37. ***Politics-Why is it that*** a large number of interviewees articulated that persons of the African-American Persuasion believe that when they increasingly become benefactors of state and federal laws unbeknown to persons of the Caucasian Persuasion, they then are moved to change laws that will severely limit their potential to gain influence and prosperity? In short, persons of the African-American Persuasion dub the actions mentioned above, especially when they are making political and financial progress as "Change the Game and Change the Rules Policy." Most African-Americans believe that the "Change the Game and Change the Rules Policy" indeed is intentional and designed to deter their progression.

38. ***Politics-Why is it that*** most interviewees expressed that most persons of the Caucasian Persuasion whose choice of words and actions are unquestionably consistent to one that is defined as racist and ethnically prejudicial, vehemently deny and detest the personal label of a racist?

39. ***Politics-Why is it that*** most interviewees expressed that most persons of the African-American Persuasion and their self-appointed leaders insist on employing outdated protest tactics in an attempt to encourage change in political and social issues? However, there is a growing number of African-Americans who believe that the aforementioned approach or means to gain attention on political and social outcomes have become predictably ineffective. They are more inclined to approach protests and conflicts through legal means which will perhaps impact their opposition financially and eliminate potential "violent behavior" from the equation as some are quick to report and label.

40. ***Politics-Why is it that*** the majority of interviewees expressed that persons who are political analysts and happen to be of the African-American Persuasion refrain from publicly exhibiting admiration for an exceptionally talented, experienced, and educated African-American political candidate for fear that their actions will be denoted as racially driven? Conversely, persons of the Caucasian Persuasion are inclined, without reservations, to express admiration for both African-American and Caucasian political candidates of equal intellect.

41. ***Politics-Why is it that*** when a few African-Americans who are in positions of power attempt to play politics centered around legitimate and legal business opportunities with business associates, old business colleagues, former employers, etc., both Caucasians and African-Americans create a whirlwind of business speculations of unethical doing? Conversely, when Caucasians exert the same power, it's considered by most to be a normal political and business practice. Working hard is not a part of the equation. The unwritten rule is "advance your friends and the hell with what others say; it will eventually end. Nevertheless, my friends and I will be financially secured." However, it becomes a major problem when African-Americans attempt to play the same game.

42. ***Politics-Why is it that*** when an African-American attempts to enter into the political arena, the individual is consistently reminded that if he or she were not of the African-American Persuasion, he or she would not have emerged as a significant candidate; however, the moment that the African-American candidate converses about his or her ethnicity, he or she is immediately denounced as playing the race card?

43. ***Politics-Why is it that*** most interviewees expressed that persons of the African-American Persuasion in Southern states who happen to be elected and appointed officials, particularly in Alabama and Mississippi, have not initiated legislation that significantly addresses child obesity to its core, especially in the African-American community? Voluminous amounts of statistical data note that health and medical conditions are inevitable and will become prevalent in the African-American communities if the matter is not addressed with expressed and deliberate emphases.

44. ***Politics-Why is it that*** most interviewees expressed that persons of the African-American Persuasion are rarely elected to key state governmental positions, i.e., lieutenant governor, state treasurer, attorney general, secretary of state, agriculture commissioner, speaker of the house, senate president pro-temp., insurance commissioner, etc.?

45. ***Politics-Why is it that*** persons of the Caucasian Persuasion are assumed to be more knowledgeable about any political or economic subject matter than persons of the African-American Persuasion? News networks interview more persons of the Caucasian Persuasion (approximately 15 to 1) more often than they interview local or national political African-American personalities. Are network ratings the driving force?

46. ***Politics-Why is it that*** most interviewees expressed that mostly uneducated either secondary or college male persons of the Caucasian Persuasion have expressed without any reservations their joy of demonizing, exhibiting total disrespect, and aggressively perpetuated depraved and vicious commentary that lacked any inkling of veracity against the past U. S. President Barack Obama? When asked why there was so much hatred, the majority of responses lacked reasons, most expressed discomfort with an African-American leading them; many feared possible retribution of the African-American male and others feared losing control.

47. ***Politics-Why is it that*** most interviewees expressed that most male persons of the African-American Persuasion do not understand why most male persons of the Caucasian Persuasion loathe (based on their actions) their interest in aggressively improving double-digit unemployment in their communities, especially in southern states, (i.e., Alabama, Arkansas, Florida, Georgia, Kentucky, Louisiana, Mississippi, North Carolina, Oklahoma, South Carolina, Tennessee, Texas, Virginia, and West Virginia)? Most male persons of the African-American Persuasion believe significant business opportunities and employment will vastly improve the quality of life in their communities, reduce crime, and increase local and state revenues. They ask, "why the reluctance?"

48. ***Politics-Why is it that*** many persons of the Caucasian Persuasion believe that persons of the African-American Persuasion are consistently unqualified to hold any office of power or significance in state government, especially in Southern states, (i.e., Alabama, Arkansas, Florida, Georgia, Kentucky, Louisiana, Mississippi, North Carolina, Oklahoma, South Carolina, Tennessee, Texas, Virginia, and West Virginia)? If an opportunity becomes a reality for an African-American to hold a state government position of power, why is it usually limited to one term or administration?

49. ***Politics-Why is it that*** persons of the Caucasian Persuasion have consistently remained in positions of power in the majority of all state elected offices in most southern states regardless of their political or ethnic constituency (persons of the African-American Persuasion)?

50. ***Politics-Why is it that*** most interviewees expressed that most uneducated male persons of the Caucasian Persuasion were more inclined to use various reasons to dislike the past U.S. President Barack Obama, particularly as frequently labeling

him as a radical, a pure socialist, non-Christian (an Arab/
Muslim practicing the religion of Islam faith), and an extreme
progressive? Why is it that the group mentioned above abhors
any policy or idea he initiates, but concurs with a welcoming
spirit, a male person of the same Caucasian Persuasion that
introduces the identical concept with perhaps a different name?

51. ***Politics-Why is it that*** the American judicial system is
disproportionally unfavorable towards persons of the
African-American Persuasion in comparison to those of the
Caucasian Persuasion in all facets of law even if their offense
is unequivocally identical? Thus, with more specificity, why
is it that more persons of the African-American Persuasion,
particularly African-American males, are indisputably
incarcerated disproportionally more than Caucasian males?

52. ***Politics-Why is it that*** most interviewees expressed that
most persons of the African-American Persuasion believe
that most persons of the Caucasian Persuasion are goaded by
the Caucasian females to unabashedly dislike the African-
American male extending from the United States first African-
American President to the average hometown teen by deliberate
and subtle actions? Such actions include, but are not limited to,
clutching their purses, alerting security or law enforcement
if one perceives that an African-American male is deemed
displaced in their neighborhoods, exit pool settings when
absorbing sun rays when an African-American male begins
to partake and enjoy the pool's tranquil setting and amenities,
and frantically lock car doors as an African-American male of
any age or stature approaches their vehicle which is adjacent
to a sidewalk or street crossing.

53. ***Politics-Why is it that*** most interviewees expressed that
most persons of the African-American Persuasion believe
that most persons of the Caucasian Persuasion consciously

or subconsciously deem African-Americans as a problem? Regardless of Caucasians' socio-economic states, (i.e., exceedingly poor or exceptionally wealthy), they believe that persons of the African-American Persuasion are not worthy by one iota to amass any substantial financial increase if it exceeds their immediate status level by one dime.

54. *Politics-Why is it that* nearly all interviewees expressed that most persons of the Caucasian Persuasion question and limit the employability of particularly African-American males and then question or despise their enrollment for government assistance?

55. *Politics-Why is it that* nearly all interviewees expressed that most persons of the Caucasian Persuasion believe that the mass majority of persons receiving government assistance (welfare) are overwhelmingly and categorically persons of the African-American Persuasion?

56. *Politics-Why is it that* nearly all interviewees expressed that most persons of the African-American Persuasion believe an overwhelmingly large percentage of state and federal legislation is frequently and consistently drafted and introduced to benefit only (economically) male persons of the Caucasian Persuasion? Most African-Americans believe when any economic piece of legislation is written, it is "always" designed to limit African-Americans considerably from partaking, but ensure that persons of the Caucasian Persuasion benefit exponentially. Additionally, most African-Americans believe state and federal legislation is written to work against their interest and to thwart their progression regardless of the ethnicity of the representative they chose to elect.

57. *Politics-Why is it that* most male legislators of the Caucasian Persuasion complain about African-American males not

working or desire to work, but author or co-author legislation that is quick to restrict or limit the African-American male educational and financial progression?

58. *Politics-Why is it that* nearly all interviewees expressed that most individuals of the African-America Persuasion legislative caucuses infrequently speak on, or draft legislation that expressly and economically benefit African-American communities? If local or state general obligation bond are issued for capital improvement projects or public/private industry incentive developments, it is highly likely persons or businesses of the African-American Persuasion will secure less than 10% of design or construction work. Most interviewees expressed that persons or businesses of the Caucasian Persuasion will be awarded 90% to 95% of all work (design, construction, manufacturing, materials, and supplies, etc.) and the bulk of "minority participation work" will be awarded to any other group including female persons or businesses of the Caucasian Persuasion.

59. *Politics-Why is it that* nearly all interviewees expressed that most people of the Caucasian Persuasion and African-Americans Persuasion believe that at least fifty percent of the African-American population is living off government assistance programs?

60. *Politics-Why is it that* nearly all interviewees expressed that most states, especially Southern states exercise every political angle to reduce African-American legislative representation and voting participation by gerrymandering political districts and requiring voter ID respectfully?

61. *Politics-Why is it tha*t nearly all interviewees expressed that the American judicial system which is governed, managed, and administered, more often than not by persons of the

Caucasian Persuasion find it resoundingly difficult to reign in the indisputable plea bargaining and sentencing structure (judges, lawyers, district attorneys, state attorneys general, state correctional commissioners, parole boards, etc.) that are purposely targeting African-American males? The interviewees further expressed, that once an African-American male pleads guilty via plea bargaining and goes through the system for a crime he did not commit, he will be stripped from local, state, and federal voting rights, federal grants for education, federal housing, and limited of any employment for several years to life. He will forever be treated as a criminal. How can a person under those clouds (falsely accused, arrested, assigned a poorly experienced public defender, encouraged to plead guilty or await trial for three to six months, cannot afford bail, sentenced, served time and released, no job, no money, no training, and dumped in same environment) of shame and torment, experience life joyfully?

62. ***Politics-Why is it that*** nearly all interviewees particularly persons of the Caucasian Persuasion expressed that the American judicial system treats an African-American male or female "thief" (one that steals $500 from a business) differently than a Caucasian male or female "embezzler" (one that steals $500,000 from a business)? Interviewees further differentiated the expedience of arrests, indictments, and sentencing of those of the African-American Persuasion vs. those of the Caucasian Persuasion. They continued to express that the differences are quite compelling and place the African-American at an alarming and dreadful disadvantage.

63. ***Politics-Why is it that*** nearly all interviewees particularly persons of the Caucasian Persuasion expressed that the American judicial system treats an African-American male or female "drug dealer" (one apprehended with 1 oz. of crack cocaine) differently than a Caucasian male or female

"recreational addict" (one apprehended with 1 oz. of powdered cocaine)? Interviewees further differentiated the expedience of arrests, indictments, and sentencing of those of the African-American Persuasion vs. those of the Caucasian Persuasion. They continued to express that the differences are quite compelling and place the African-American at an alarming and dreadful disadvantage.

64. ***Politics-Why is it that*** nearly all interviewees particularly persons of the Caucasian Persuasion expressed that the American judicial system treats an African-American male or female "gangster or thug" (one apprehended for toting and firing a gun) differently than a Caucasian male or female "self-defender" (one apprehended for toting and firing a gun)? Interviewees further differentiated the expedience of arrests, indictments, and sentencing of those of the African-American Persuasion vs. those of the Caucasian Persuasion. They continued to express that the differences are quite compelling and place the African-American at an alarming and dreadful disadvantage.

Chapter 3
Education

Education

Education is the means to the potential growth of any community. It plays a pivotal role in securing the prospective grasp of prosperity in the lives of any community people. It also imparts wisdom and wisdom imparts power which is synonymous with influence. The African-American and Caucasian communities understand the importance of having a solid education. Both ethnicities believe the introduction to reading is incredibly significant at ages 2-3, knowing the fact that it is essential to ascertaining knowledge, helps in decoding, potentially improves social and emotional aptitude, enhances comprehension, and heightens creativity. If the above advantages are noted as necessities for any community to develop well-rounded and articulate pre-school children and subsequently intelligent teens and adults, why is there such an enormous divide and profound disparities between the African-American and Caucasian communities? Access to education in recent years has been considered relatively easy, but surprisingly statistics dictate otherwise, primarily in the inner city African-American communities.

Inner-city African-American families, who are desirous of securing a good education for their children in hopes of building a strong intellectual foundation, believe that a sound education would introduce opportunities they otherwise would not have had the chance to experience. Many African-American families have capitalized on the rare and slim opportunities that are available in inner-city school districts. African-Americans and Caucasians who do not reside in the inner-city or do not have children in the public school system ask why inner-city children are not receiving a quality education when the government (our tax dollars) provides them all the tools they need. Many express that their tax dollars should be sufficient for any child to receive an adequate education.

Pouring more money into the system will not improve the inner-city children's academic levels. Some say the facilities are old, but they are entirely adequate to provide an acceptable learning environment.

Interviewees who expressed the harsher sentiments as to why inner-city communities and their children are constantly complaining about the lack of funding and receiving a decent education happen to be of the Caucasian Persuasion. The majority interviewees of said ethnic group did not reside in inner-city school districts and had alternate private academic establishments to send their children. Some made conscious efforts to relocate to suburban communities or adjacent school districts to just remove their children from the inner-city school district and remove their tax dollars as well.

This chapter depicts the multiple educational related issues that have become paramount in recent years as shared by both ethnic groups in secondary and higher education systems. African-Americans and Caucasian Americans both desire the same objective, (i.e., quality education, access to technology, and resources that can help promote cognitive thinking, and advance intellect). Both believe education is essential to establish solid positions in a competitive global marketplace. However, each ethnic group is taking separate and non-complementary approaches in an attempt to achieve said objectives. African-American interviewees believe Caucasian Americans have such an enormous advantage over them by ensuring their legislative, corporate, and financial exclusion. African-Americans believe if they have to ask daily or garner the Caucasian American knob of approval for anything, they are by definition at a significant disadvantage in all facets of education. The following questions represent the majority of interviewees and my observations.

Educational Observations / Differences

Don't Look Now, But Equal Educational Gains Are In Question

1. *Educational-Why is it that* it is more prevalent for female persons of the African-American Persuasion who work in academic settings and hold EdDs or PhDs to have a tendency to over-enunciate the "King's English?"

2. *Educational-Why is it that* nearly all interviewees expressed that persons of the African-American and Caucasian Persuasions learn of a presidency vacancy at an institution of higher learning, (i.e., colleges or universities), only consider submitting their application to the institution that has demographics largely of their same persuasion, regardless of their impeccable credentials?

3. *Educational-Why is it that* when most Historically Black Colleges and Universities (HBCUs) receive large endowments become recognized for advanced research, host a world-renowned lecture series, and host any other noted services, most persons in the Caucasian community have less than a penny's worth of interest? However, if all of the above activities were associated with Predominantly White Institutions (PWIs), the public interest becomes heightened, and local papers proudly contribute to amplifying and broadening community awareness.

4. *Educational-Why is it that* most interviewees believe the poorest and smallest PWIs are notably more physically maintained and aesthetically developed than the poorest and smallest HBCUs?

5. *Educational-Why is it that* male and female persons of the African-American Persuasion of all ages who are members of Greek fraternities or sororities consistently and proudly display their affiliation paraphernalia, (i.e., car tags, clothing apparel, libation mugs, notebooks, Greek colors, etc.), more so than that of persons of the Caucasian Persuasion who also have Greek affiliations?

6. *Educational-Why is it that* nearly all interviewees expressed that most persons of the Caucasian Persuasion and a large portion of the African-American Persuasion believe that most Caucasians are innately brighter academically than persons of the African-American Persuasion, even if their actions deem them incompetent or completely clueless?

7. *Educational-Why is it that* most persons of the Caucasian Persuasion consistently equate persons of the African-American Persuasion as ones who are never academically qualified to do mostly anything, administer or manage any project, perform any task or provide leadership of any kind, but believe if they are hired, there is always a person of the Caucasian Persuasion that has missed out on an opportunity and also is more qualified?

8. *Educational-Why is it that* most persons of the Caucasian Persuasion consistently express the evils of affirmative action and frequently allude to or establish an inference that persons of the African-American Persuasion do not deserve job opportunities until all persons of the Caucasian Persuasion have been provided an opportunity first?

9. *Educational-Why is it that* nearly all interviewees expressed that most persons of the Caucasian Persuasion consistently score higher on exams than African-Americans when vying for civil work positions, (i.e., post office workers, law enforcement officers, firefighters, air traffic controller, etc.)?

Most interviewees expressly believe that most examinees who happen to be of the Caucasian Persuasion are privy to examination strategies and inside knowledge as compared to persons who happen to be of the African-American Persuasion. Additionally, most interviewees explicitly believe the historical ethnicity of the employer is often dominated by persons of their own ethnicity and will promote the employment of Caucasians more often unreservedly.

10. *Educational-Why is it that* nearly all interviewees expressed that most persons of the Caucasian Persuasion dangerously believe that regardless of the advanced education persons of the African-American Persuasion receive or the institution they may attend or have attended, they are not as qualified for various positions simply because there is always a person of the Caucasian Persuasion that is more qualified? Most interviewees believe a cloud of unending reservations hovers over most newly hired African-Americans indefinitely.

11. *Educational-Why is it that* most media outlets only showcase and designate persons of the African-American Persuasion (experts in Black studies) if there is dissension between self-appointed African-American leaders, but rarely showcase experts in science, foreign affairs, language, history, political science, etc.?

12. *Educational-Why is it that* most secondary and higher education institutions that have a majority African-American population do not emphasize the importance of taking ACT and SAT standardized exams as frequently as possible or provide multiple mock exams to ease test anxiety significantly and improve test scores?

13. *Educational-Why is it that* most middle and high school Caucasian students are strongly encouraged and understand the

importance of taking the ACT and SAT as early and often as possible to improve test scores to gain entrance to prestigious colleges and universities? On the contrary, African-Americans are not zealously encouraged or frequently informed to take advantage of same practice?

14. *Educational-Why is it that* nearly all interviewees expressed that most persons of the African-American Persuasion rarely document their narratives of life experiences and lack the notion of putting them in a written or audible format for future generations?

15. *Educational-Why is it that* radio and television talk show personalities who happen to be of the Caucasian Persuasion have a tendency to incite intra-ethnic dissension on issues that are primarily and extensively discussed in the African-American communities?

16. *Educational-Why is it that* the majority of interviewees expressed that African-American adult males have failed the African-American community by allowing the bond and strength of the family to be broken? Most African-American males have permitted inconsequential priorities, (i.e., material articles, street pharmaceutical distribution, quick money, lascivious endeavors, etc.) to plague their communities, but failed to provide leadership in family values, education, personal responsibility, business, economics, and politics? A substantial number of African-American males are not informed or encouraged to understand the subjects as mentioned earlier matters. Where are the African-American male mentors? Yes, there are successfully organized mentoring programs and organizations throughout the country, but the question remains, where are the ordinary community individuals or non-organized neighborhood African-American mentors?

Your Educational Future And Opportunities Are Different

17. *Educational-Why is it that* most Historically Black Colleges and Universities place very little emphases on encouraging African-American males to enter the field of education, especially when the need is overwhelming? Additionally, are young African-American males more desirous of having a strong and smart African-American male figure in their lives to lead and love them unconditionally?

18. *Educational-Why is it that* most middle and high school African-American male students do not have a strong desire or aspiration to perform well in school in comparison to most Caucasian male students? Studies have rendered positive results that African-American male students are more than capable of advancing with honors to college, but sadly, in most cases, friends and family do not provide the support and encouragement they need to want to excel?

19. *Educational-Why is it that* the majority of interviewees expressed that most adult African-American males and females are not demanding that their offspring, relatives, or mentees aspire to enter the fields of accounting, architecture, medicine, law, and engineering? It has been proven on numerous occasions that male and female African-Americans can excel astoundingly in said fields if more emphases are placed on Science, Technology, Engineering, and Math (STEM) fields at an early age.

20. *Educational-Why is it that* most public and private Historically Black Colleges and Universities are still experiencing enormous financial disparities in comparison to Predominantly White Institutions of equal size?

21. *Educational-Why is it that* the majority of interviewees expressed that most male and female persons of the African-American

Persuasion who are members of Greek fraternities or sororities consistently and proudly display their affiliation paraphernalia on car tags but in most cases do not provide a hint as to where they attended college? Does their fraternity or sorority play a more important role in their lives than the four-year educational institution they attended that provided them the opportunity to participate in the eight to twelve weeks pledging exercise? Additionally, does the Greek affiliation out weight the alumni status of each participate and is each participant socially defined by the perception of the organization or is the organization defined by each participant's principles and character?

22. *Educational-Why is it that* the majority of interviewees expressed that most male and female persons of the Caucasian Persuasion who are members of Greek fraternities or sororities rarely display their affiliation paraphernalia via their car tags, but proudly exhibit their alma mater through sanctioned vehicle accessories to the general public?

23. *Educational-Why is it that* a large portion of African-American parents recognize that many of their children do not master math and science at a level that is expected, but most of them never consider establishing private schools or academies with high emphases in said subjects? Why is it that each HBCU does not have math and science laboratory schools at the elementary, middle or high school levels?

24. *Educational-Why is it that* most middle and high school African-American males and females believe being smart or making exceptional grades is not cool?

25. *Educational-Why is it that* the majority of interviewees expressed that most Caucasians and African-American school teachers and administrators are not taking advantage of the incredible memory talent most African-American students

have when it is applied to pop or rap music lyrics? It is a given that most African-American students have the ability to learn and recite anything. Will a simple change in instruction bring out the brilliance of said population?

26. ***Educational-Why is it that*** most HBCUs do not sponsor internships, language, architecture, engineering, literature, foreign, and economic studies abroad for global exposure, similar to those done by PWIs?

27. ***Educational-Why is it that*** nearly all interviewees expressed that most African-Americans need to have a greater level of education to be simply considered for most job opportunities more so than persons of the Caucasian Persuasion?

28. ***Educational-Why is it that*** nearly all interviewees expressed that most students of the Caucasian and African-American Persuasions who attend desegregated secondary schools and institutions of higher learning segregate themselves in most social functions and campus dining settings?

29. ***Educational-Why is it that*** nearly all interviewees expressed that most students of the Caucasian and African-American Persuasions who attend desegregated secondary schools and institutions of higher learning subconsciously believe that every instance where the different race is elected or chosen for any position or school representation, an undercurrent of racial preference is the driving force?

30. ***Educational-Why is it that*** nearly all interviewees expressed that most persons of both the Caucasian and African-American Persuasions who attend PWIs assume without indecisiveness that all African-American attendees are academically inferior, poor, raised in a broken home, and are receiving some form of financial aid?

31. ***Educational-Why is it that*** nearly all interviewees expressed that most persons of the Caucasian Persuasion frown on the idea that their tax dollars are earmarked for grants and other federal financial aid programs for African-Americans and ignore the fact that more Caucasians benefit and enjoy favor from such programs?

Study Hard, Work Hard, And Win – Ersatz Concept

32. ***Educational-Why is it that*** nearly all interviewees expressed that male persons of the Caucasian Persuasion are more inclined to commit multiple shootings in mostly Caucasian-populated rural and suburban academic settings filled with innocent and unarmed victims more so than male persons of the African-American Persuasion? In most cases, the Caucasian males carrying out such an act vividly provide clues and emphatically state that they will spray the school with bullets and end the lives of several administrators, staff, and classmates because they felt wronged or denied social acceptance.

33. ***Educational-Why is it that*** nearly all interviewees expressed that most persons of the Caucasian Persuasion do not handle rejection as well as most persons of the African-American Persuasion when vying for acceptance to Ivy League institutions of higher learning? Most Caucasians who have been rejected defined themselves as failures and find it tough to motivate themselves to seek other institutions and educational alternatives.

34. ***Educational-Why is it that*** nearly all interviewees expressed that most educators of the African-American Persuasion are not outraged over the myth or fact that there is a greater percent of African-American males incarcerated than those attending college and male parental leadership in the African-American community is nearly non-existent? Where is the outrage and infuriation among the more mature adult African-American males?

35. ***Educational-Why is it that*** nearly all interviewees expressed that most persons of the African-American Persuasion who serve as president, vice president, associate vice president, dean, assistant dean, department chair, and other upper-level positions at Historically Black Colleges and Universities happen to possess a light-skinned complexion? This continuous social subconscious phenomenon is extended with greater intensity at Predominantly White Institutions.

36. ***Educational-Why is it that*** nearly all interviewees expressed that most persons of the Caucasian Persuasion who evaluate college entry applications can categorize and conclude with impressive precision which applicants are African-American by name only and then control the percentage of minority college acceptance? This practice is exercised not only with students that are vying for college acceptance at Predominantly White Institutions but also for college instructional and administrative positions as well.

37. ***Educational-Why is it that*** most Historically Black Colleges and Universities that recruit mostly African-American students and all of whom have majored in architecture, engineering, computer science, and other technical fields, rarely follow-up on the employment status or national professional certification of their alumni? Most do not provide mock exams to help ease exam anxiety and ensure a notable success rate for their alumni, especially when it is a given that most students have not been exposed to their perspective field as elementary, junior high, and high school students.

38. ***Educational-Why is it that*** most Historically Black Colleges and Universities that recruit and graduate mostly African-American students who have expressed interest and majored in architecture, engineering, computer science, and other technical fields, rarely secure professional design service contracts from

these graduates, even after they have gained twenty or more years of experience? Most southern HBCUs obtain other ethnic groups to provide professional service contracts.

39. ***Educational-Why is it that*** most Historically Black Colleges and Universities do not demonstrate any confidence in their architectural, engineering, computer science, and other technical field alumni even after gaining twenty years of valuable experience? When questioned about the use of their alumni to render sizeable projects, they will provide a myriad of excuses not to hire them, but will quickly hire any other ethnic group with little knowledge of their community dispositions and who may not have the university's best interest at heart.

40. ***Educational-Why is it that*** most Predominantly White Institutions demonstrate full support and confidence in their architectural, engineering, and computer science graduates, but will find every excuse not to hire an African-American firm for any project of significant size? However, the same colleges and universities will allow African-Americans only to serve a subordinate role in a limited capacity, (i.e., sub-consultant or sub-contractor, but not a prime contractor).

41. ***Educational-Why is it that*** most interviewees expressed that persons of both African-American and Caucasian Persuasions believe that educating a child as a parent primarily hinges on the acute interest of "giving a damn" about them? If one (a parent or parents) does not participate in the child's learning process or does not exhibit one iota of interest, the child, parent, community, and country lose. Understanding the logic mentioned above, why is it that the lack of participation and interest are prevalent in most African-American communities?

42. ***Educational-Why is it that*** most interviewees expressed that persons of the African-American Persuasion consistently criticize persons of the Caucasian Persuasion for most of their missed opportunities in education, business, and the erosion of community and social values? Who should take the brunt of the blame presently and historically?

43. *Educational-Why is it that* most interviewees expressed that persons of the Caucasian Persuasion consistently criticize persons of the African-Americans Persuasion for most of their missed opportunities in education, business, and erosion of community and social values? Who should take the brunt of the blame presently and historically?

44. *Educational-Why is it that* most interviewees expressed that most persons of the Caucasian Persuasion who receive primary and secondary education from private academy schools assume that individuals of the African-American Persuasion who also attend the same private academy school are voucher recipients or question how can they afford this kind of education?

45. *Educational-Why is it that* the majority of interviewees expressed that most persons who are administrators at private or chartered schools with dominant Caucasian demographics have a tendency to reprimand frequently more African-American males who constitute less than .01 percent of the school's population? It is also observed that if a female of the Caucasian Persuasion utters the idea that a male African-American brushed up against her, it will be deemed harassment and the reprimand begins even if it is done unintentionally.

46. *Educational-Why is it that* the majority of interviewees expressed that most persons of the Caucasian Persuasion are more inclined to encourage and place significant emphases on the importance of reading to their offspring more so than persons of the African-American Persuasion?

47. ***Educational-Why is it that*** the majority of interviewees expressed that most persons of the Caucasian Persuasion do not take advantage of the minority status as a student at Historically Black Colleges and Universities? Said status invites free or significant tuition, room and board reductions, classroom accommodations, and advantages they would not otherwise receive at Predominantly White Institutions. Why purposely avoid legitimate and open opportunities?

48. ***Educational-Why is it that*** the majority of interviewees expressed that most persons of the African-American Persuasion are labeled in an uncomplimentary way when they take advantage of the minority status as a student at Predominantly White Institutions? Said status invites free or significant tuition, room and board reductions, classroom accommodations, and advantages they would not otherwise receive at Historically Black Colleges and Universities. Why the uncomplimentary and belittling label?

49. ***Educational-Why is it that*** most Historically Black Colleges and Universities do not frequently mandate an audience with their African-American males to explicitly and unapologetically discuss political, education, social, judicial, business, and relationship matters with them? Most Historically Black Colleges and Universities are vehemently aware of the unpleasant and disturbing statistics of the African-American male. Society has consistently characterized them as dangerous, unmanageable, lackadaisical, violent, products of fatherlessness, female exploiters, destructive, and much more demeaning labels and objectionable characteristics.

50. ***Educational-Why is it that*** most Historically Black Colleges and Universities do not frequently mandate an audience with their African-American females to explicitly and unapologetically discuss political, education, social, judicial, business, and relationship matters with them? Most Historically Black Colleges and Universities are vehemently aware of the unpleasant and disturbing statistics of the African-American female. Society has consistently characterized them as loose cannons, disrespectful, unmanageable, lackadaisical, products of fatherlessness, drama queens, promiscuous, and much more demeaning labels and objectionable characteristics.

51. *Educational-Why is it that* most Historically Black Colleges and Universities publically solicit "Minority Owned" enterprises to do business on their campuses? Conversely, most Predominantly White Institutions do not publicly solicit "Majority Owned" enterprises to do work on their campuses. It's a given. Why are most Historically Black Colleges and Universities leery, hesitant, and fearful of doing business with professional businesspersons of the African-American Persuasion regardless of the years they have been in business if work required is over ten million dollars, but will welcome a joint venture if the partnering team is of the Caucasian Persuasion? It seems as though the universities breathe a sigh of relief once the Caucasian team is on board.

52. *Educational-Why is it that* most Historically Black Colleges and Universities have managed to produce scholars and various professionals, but are not acknowledged in national media outlets that perhaps would heighten awareness to other persuasions and possibly secure larger endowments?

53. *Educational-Why is it that* the majority of interviewees expressed that most persons of the Caucasian Persuasion are for the African-American community establishing charter schools or private academies if they receive quarterly expenditure records for the public funded charter schools and do not have to provide any funding for the private academies? Both ethnic group interviewees continued to express that if the

African-American charter school or private academy students participated in (attended by 95% African-Americans) state required skill tests, ACT, or SAT and their scores exceed their expectations or surpass other Caucasian charter and private academies (attended by 95% Caucasians); local, state, and perhaps federal inquiries will be launched for possible test tampering. Admittedly, both ethnic groups expressed their views on the scenario as mentioned above because of learned low academic expectations of African-American students.

54. ***Educational-Why is it that*** the majority of interviewees expressed, as an example that most large Southeastern (SEC) public Predominantly White Institutions established between 1785 to 1878 main athletic program (football) is today's principal student recruiting mechanism? Why is it that they have the largest single campus auxiliary budgets ranging from $62 million dollars to $143 million dollars, in command of an estimated $527 million dollars in revenues collectively for the fiscal year 2014-2015, they have some of the highest paid staff, most improved modern facilities, practice aggressively recruitment of a large percentage of African-American players, and have approximately a fourteen percent share of African-American head football coaches, but have not entertained the inspiration of selecting an African-American president individually? Some interviewees expanded their reasoning behind the question, to simply say, the football athletic "financial engine" has the most powerful voice on campus and with a strong alumni, an African-American president's control and power will be similar to existing Caucasian presidential authority; so why not.

Chapter 4
Community Environment

Community Environment

This chapter embodies observations of idiosyncrasies that are particularly unique to African-Americans and Caucasian Americans community environments. Both ethnic groups offer interesting inquiries about each other. The listing is not a compilation of just a few individuals or a small group but is a collection of multiple individuals and groups throughout the country. Surprisingly, all interviewees lowered their wall of defense to speak on various issues with sincerity and without hesitation. I found that the majority of interviewees were pleasantly comfortable sharing their observations, beliefs, and dubious values of the opposing ethnic group. Interviewees enthusiastically expressed the need to "put it out there" because people of both ethnic groups do not have a clue as to why persons of the African-American and Caucasian Persuasion do what they do. Most of the interviewees believe that this is the most opportune time to speak on and inquire about many race issues, particularly ones between African-Americans and Caucasian Americans daily experience.

This chapter perhaps may be one of the liveliest depictions of subtle and immensely noticeable idiosyncrasies of African-Americans and Caucasian Americans. The previous and subsequent chapters are just as lively, but are more concentrated and speak primarily to each subject matter. The inquiry listing is undeniably the largest compilation of all chapters. Each question has generated at least one-hundred similar observations and scenarios which encouraged its placement in my book. My interpretation of all persons and groups who were interviewed is that they are elated that someone has compiled a listing of questions each ethnic group wanted to ask or find answers to but didn't want to appear bias. Actions of either ethnic group are not deemed negative or positive. They are simply thoughts, beliefs, practices, learned behavior, sub-cultural exercises, and sub-cultural survival antics that are widespread in their communities.

The community environment covers a wide variety of subjects. Instead of having multiple subtitles, I opted to place the interviewees' and my broad range of inquiring interest in this chapter. One may find that the series of queries may cause a sudden physical desire to display comedic outbursts (or laughter). On the other hand, one may find themselves besieged by humility, potential disagreement, and conceivably resentment. This array of emotions is to be expected. But those who project vehement unseemly displeasure in digesting the observations and beliefs of thousands of African-Americans and Caucasian Americans and yours truly may require in-depth self-examination. Please recognize these views are the beliefs and experiences of thousands of people and do not define a particular ethnic group in its totality. Yes, each ethnic group is comprised of millions of individuals with their way of thinking, different socio-economic status, varied educational levels, mixed political views and affiliations, and countless other distinctions. Each individual is associated with and characterized as either African-American or Caucasian American. These two distinctive ethnicities can and have created exceptional children (Mulattos) who are often quite attractive and have an array of other appealing attributes. Although the offspring share the gene pool of both ethnicities, their exterior features are usually described as those most similar to those of the African-American Persuasion. Thus, society more often than not defines or views them as African-Americans. While all of the above interpretations of individualism exist among each ethnicity, the social structure corrals all individualism into one group and is frequently defined by one's pigmentation. These represent the majority of my interviewees and my observations.

Community Environment
Observations / Differences

This Can't Be Real

1. *Community Environment-Why is it that* the majority of interviewees expressed that most persons of the African-American Persuasion who happen to be thieves, frequently steal from other African-Americans? This act of thievery is usually performed within their communities approximately one mile from their residence, and the average cost of the stolen property excluding cars is less than $1,500.00.

2. *Community Environment-Why is it that* the majority of interviewees expressed that most persons of the African-American Persuasion who happen to be thieves, more often steal from other African-Americans and are less likely to steal from homes and businesses of the Caucasian Persuasion, even when their valuables are openly exposed or entirely visible?

3. *Community Environment-Why is it that* the majority of interviewees expressed that most persons of the African-American Persuasion remove any and all potential possibilities of viewing (drawn curtains and blinds) the interior spaces of their homes from passersby, (i.e., great room, dining room, kitchen, den or living room) at dusk? Frequent observances reveal that most persons of the Caucasian Persuasion allow a passerby to view (without drawn curtains or blinds) openly several interior spaces of their homes at dusk and late hours of the evening.

4. *Community Environment-Why is it that* the majority of interviewees expressed that most persons of the African-American Persuasion with an active child or active children

privately and publicly bellow out that their child is or children are just "BAD," with the absence of providing consistent positive and constructive emotional reinforcement?

5. ***Community Environment-Why is it that*** the majority of interviewees expressed that most males of the African-American Persuasion between the ages of 17 and 35 years old drive cars with the driver's seat in the 45° reclining position and if cruising with another male of the same persuasion, his seat is also in the 45° or greater reclining position with the absence of the use of a seat belt?

6. ***Community Environment-Why is it that*** the majority of interviewees expressed that most young males of the African-American Persuasion who own work dogs are more inclined to have dogs that are considered vicious and aggressive, (i.e., Pit Bull, Rottweiler or Mastiff)?

7. ***Community Environment-Why is it that*** most interviewees of the African-American Persuasion expressed that most males of the Caucasian Persuasion, who consider themselves cowboys that project the image of being tough guys, wear extremely tight fitting denim jeans proudly displaying their front and rear features, unlike the average male of the African-American Persuasion?

8. ***Community Environment-Why is it that*** a substantial amount of television music videos that feature male artists of the African-American Persuasion have alluring and ravishingly attractive females of all persuasions donned in two-piece swimsuits, halters, ultra miniskirts or mini pants, but the musical artist and his male entourage are fully clothed and are donned in two to three layers of clothing even if the set is centered around a swimming pool, beach or summer activities?

9. ***Community Environment-Why is it that*** television music videos that feature male artists of the Caucasian Persuasion do not expose the vilest and demeaning sexuality of Caucasian females? Why do most Caucasian and African-American male and female interviewees seem to believe that some African-American male rap artists searched the deepest perverted gutters looking for the most "vulgar dancing" African-American females that they could find exploiting and degrading them in their music videos just to promote a sound track?

10. ***Community Environment-Why is it that*** the majority of interviewees expressed that most males of the Caucasian Persuasion, who are awarded multimillion dollar athletic or music contracts, immediately purchase expensive antique vehicles, very little jewelry and clothing, invest in real estate, the stock market, long-standing mutual funds, or other long-standing profitable business ventures? All such purchases are unlike those of most male persons of the African-American Persuasion. They frequently seem to purchase short-term and tangible items, i.e., guns, dogs, escort services, expensive cars, jewelry, clothes, and display rolls of cash.

11. ***Community Environment-Why is it that*** the majority of interviewees expressed that most males of the African-American Persuasion who are awarded or have signed multimillion dollar athletic or music contracts, immediately purchase extremely expensive and large gold, silver, diamond, or platinum neck chains, watches, rings, and earrings in lieu of investing in the ownership of professional football, basketball, baseball, and hockey teams, real estate, long standing mutual funds, or other long-standing profitable businesses?

12. ***Community Environment-Why is it that*** the majority of interviewees expressed that most young persons of the African-American Persuasion twelve to twenty-five years old are more

impressed and in awe of another African-American with a new polished car equipped with custom chrome rims than that of the purchase of a new 6,000 to 8,000 square feet home? Yet, the reverse enthusiasm is displayed by persons of the Caucasian Persuasion who have secured similar properties.

13. *Community Environment-Why is it that* the majority of interviewees expressed that most persons of the Caucasian Persuasion, when using public toilet facilities, seldom wash their hands upon completion of doing their business, while most persons of the African-American Persuasion wash and sanitize their hands more consistently after the use of public toilet facilities?

14. *Community Environment-Why is it that* the majority of interviewees expressed that most married female persons of the Caucasian Persuasion who have multiple births, (i.e., triplets, quadruplets, quintuplets, sextuplets, or more) by way of artificial insemination are nationally lauded, inundated with accolades, and given gifts and significant financial support? Notwithstanding, married female persons of the African-American Persuasion who have natural multiple births are rarely acknowledged and certainly are not offered equivalent or significant financial support.

15. *Community Environment-Why is it that* a number of male law enforcement persons who happen to be of the Caucasian Persuasion, consistently exercise marksmanship on young and mature male persons of the African-American Persuasion that result in death, are invariably exonerated for their actions?

16. *Community Environment-Why is it that* tort reform is being heavily considered and adopted especially in states where present day court hearings/trials are held in predominantly African-American communities? Thus, the majority of jurors

are of the African-American Persuasion and awards are usually greater than those issued in communities where jurors are of the Caucasian Persuasion.

17. ***Community Environment-Why is it that*** the majority of interviewees expressed that most juvenile runaways are persons of the Caucasian Persuasion, especially when statistics conclude that said persons have exceptional opportunities to become productive citizens, unlike juvenile persons of the African-American Persuasion for whom societal opinion clearly forecasts bleak opportunities and poor economic expectancies?

18. ***Community Environment-Why is it that*** the majority of interviewees expressed that most male rap artists of the African-American Persuasion, who are highly overweight, aesthetically and communicatively challenged, and "want-to-be thugs," feature attractive female African-American dancers in their videos, but exploit and demoralize them in their music to the degree of portraying them as common street prostitutes?

19. ***Community Environment-Why is it that*** the majority of interviewees expressed that most male persons of the Caucasian Persuasion between the ages of 15-30 years old hardly ever don what is deemed Historically Black Colleges and Universities' paraphernalia or athletic sports gear? Conversely, male persons of the African-American Persuasion proudly don paraphernalia and sports gear of Predominantly White Institutions, even if they have never seen nor have a clue as to their demographics or geographical locations.

20. ***Community Environment-Why is it that*** the majority of interviewees expressed that most male and female persons of the African-American Persuasion are more often required to stand in long lines to conduct business in financial institutions, grocery stores, super stories, residence utility payment centers,

and pharmacies that are located in their community due to lack of adequate personnel? Persons of the Caucasian Persuasion are not usually subjected to standing in long lines in their communities as often as persons of the African-American Persuasion. Is this because an adequate personnel is often provided?

21. ***Community Environment-Why is it that*** the majority of interviewees expressed that most male persons of the African-American Persuasion purchase extra audio and electronic equipment (i.e., DVD players) in both front and rear seats, oversized woofers, equalizers, etc., for their cars or SUVs for the purpose of having entertainment on long distance travel, comfort, and convenience, but rarely travel thirty miles beyond the city limits in which they live? Why the major expense?

22. ***Community Environment-Why is it that*** the majority of interviewees expressed that most persons of the African-American Persuasion are more critical of another African-American, especially when one is recognized for business, fashion, sports, education, literary, and entertainment achievements?

23. ***Community Environment-Why is it that*** the majority of interviewees expressed that most persons of the Caucasian Persuasion deliberately discount the educational wisdom and pecuniary life worth of persons of the African-American Persuasion?

24. ***Community Environment-Why is it that*** the majority of interviewees expressed that most persons of the Caucasian Persuasion are more aggressive and adamant to encourage racial profiling or acute preconceptions, especially when the subject happens to be African-American? This pugnacious enthusiasm is heightened when a crime has been committed,

and the assailant is at large, allegedly an African-American, and has not been apprehended.

25. *Community Environment-Why is it that* the majority of interviewees expressed that mostly male persons of the Caucasian Persuasion are overwhelmingly more likely to commit extremely abhorrent, heinous, and callous crimes than male persons of the African-American Persuasion, but are never labeled as animals, monsters, or evil persons? Instead, said persons are diagnosed as having suffered from work-related mental stress disorder, bipolar disorder, schizophrenia, or oppositional defiant disorder.

26. *Community Environment-Why is it that* the majority of interviewees expressed that most persons of the Caucasian Persuasion vehemently and passionately oppose reparations to persons of the African-American Persuasion when statistically (if monetary compensation is exchanged) it has been examined that "the dollar" circulates less than two times in the African-American community? Thus, all funds hypothetically that may be issued to persons of the African-American Persuasion will inevitably be exchanged in circulation within the Caucasian Community at least nine times. Therefore, whatever is legislatively authorized regarding reparations, the bulk of all funds committed will eventually travel back to and park in the Caucasian community and help them advance their net worth.

27. *Community Environment-Why is it that* the majority of interviewees expressed that most female persons of the Caucasian Persuasion can easily imply or allude to law enforcement authorities that an African-American male is responsible for any public disruption or crime, and said authorities immediately accept their statement as infallible with little apprehension, evidence, or reservations?

28. ***Community Environment-Why is it that*** the majority of interviewees expressed that female persons of the Caucasian Persuasion are more involved in high school, college, and professional cheerleader competition activities significantly more so than persons of the African-American Persuasion?

29. ***Community Environment-Why is it that*** the majority of interviewees expressed that most female persons of the Caucasian Persuasion between the ages of 20-60 who dine in casual dining restaurants sit with their legs either tucked, crossed at the ankle or knee, or folded underneath their posterior? Frequent observances reveal that most female persons of the African-American Persuasion usually sit with their feet placed firmly on the floor or only crossed at the ankle.

30. ***Community Environment-Why is it that*** most of the interviewees expressed that most male and female persons of the Caucasian Persuasion between the ages of 15–60, when dining out in a public restaurant and while completing their entrée, blow their noses or inconspicuously remove phlegm from their throats at the table or during their exit from the restaurant? However, these acts are usually not done in upscale restaurants. Interviewees continued to ask, why is it that most African-Americans refrain from engaging in what they deem odious acts?

31. ***Community Environment-Why is it that*** most of the interviewees expressed that most male and female persons of the Caucasian Persuasion of all ages, when dining out in a public restaurant frequently wipe their noses, fling their hair, cough, talk over each other, and allow their young boy or girl to roam around and among other restaurant patrons freely with the absence of respecting other guests personal spaces? However, these acts are usually not done in upscale restaurants. But, why is it that most African-Americans refrain from engaging in such acts.

32. ***Community Environment-Why is it that*** most of the interviewees expressed that most male and female persons of the Caucasian Persuasion, when discussing a negative situation with an African-American about another African-American, make it clear that the person they are discussing is an African-American instead of addressing said person as male or female; why does race become the subject?

33. ***Community Environment-Why is it that*** most of the interviewees expressed that most female persons of the Caucasian Persuasion feel the need to have an African-American female to escort them in social settings that are attended predominantly by African-Americans?

34. ***Community Environment-Why is it that*** most of the interviewees expressed that most female children of the Caucasian Persuasion rarely display their liking or ownership of an African-American doll of a fictional character publicly? Frequent observances make known that female children of the African-American Persuasion will display their liking or ownership of any doll of the Caucasian Persuasion publicly.

35. ***Community Environment-Why is it that*** most of the interviewees expressed that most persons of the African-American Persuasion have a tendency to chastise their children publicly more so than persons of the Caucasian Persuasion? Persons on the lower end of the economic ladder and of the lower-middle socioeconomic status most commonly engage in this form of psychological discipline.

36. ***Community Environment-Why is it that*** most of the interviewees expressed that most persons of the Caucasian

Persuasion describe a considerable amount of female Caucasian actresses as drop dead gorgeous, stunningly beautiful, exquisitely appealing, incredibly alluring, and extraordinarily ravishing regardless of the low level of attractiveness they may possess? Notwithstanding, female persons of the African-American Persuasion are hardly ever described as drop dead gorgeous, stunningly beautiful, etc., regardless of how naturally attractive they may be.

37. ***Community Environment-Why is it that*** most of the interviewees expressed that senior persons of the African-American Persuasion have a handsome assembly of wall mounted portraits of Jesus Christ, Martin Luther King, Jr., John F. Kennedy, or Robert F. Kennedy in their homes mounted as closely to the ceiling as physically possible?

38. ***Community Environment-Why is it that*** most of the interviewees expressed that most female African-American comedians are considered obese?

39. ***Community Environment-Why is it that*** most of the interviewees expressed that most popular male and female African-American gospel artist considered obese?

40. ***Community Environment-Why is it that*** so few male and female persons of the Caucasian Persuasion that have the talent and attributes to become exceptional gospel singers, but choose to engage in other classes of music or are they discouraged from pursuing said genre of music?

41. ***Community Environment-Why is it that*** so few male and female persons of the African-American Persuasion that have the talent and attributes to become exceptional folk and country singers, but choose to engage in other classes of music or are they discouraged from pursuing said genre of music?

42. ***Community Environment-Why is it that*** most of the interviewees expressed that most male persons of the Caucasian Persuasion have a tendency to park at a buffet serving station and use their fingers to eat out of various trays instead of using provided plates, toothpicks or utensils? This act is consistently performed after they have shaken everybody's hand, scratched their groin area, wiped their nose, toyed with their hair, and have used public restroom facilities.

43. ***Community Environment-Why is it that*** most of the interviewees expressed that most persons of the Caucasian Persuasion are rarely recognized as "The First Caucasian" to be appointed in political, educational, sports, or business posts in predominantly African-American communities? Conversely, African-Americans are consistently recognized as "The First African-American" to hold various political, educational, sports, or business positions in predominantly Caucasian communities.

44. ***Community Environment-Why is it that*** a startling number of African-Americans disregard states laws requiring one to use car seat belts during daily travel routines? It is expressly alarming when their toddlers are not fastened in as well.

45. ***Community Environment-Why is it that*** most of the interviewees expressed that most persons of the African-American Persuasion appear to have a greater percentage of pride in their daily business and casual clothing attire than most persons of the Caucasian Persuasion?

Are You Serious?

46. ***Community Environment-Why is it that*** most of the interviewees expressed that female persons of the Caucasian Persuasion are overwhelmingly attracted to permitting their

child to participate in children pageants more so than female persons of the African-American Persuasion?

47. ***Community Environment-Why is it that*** most of the interviewees expressed that most persons of the African-American Persuasion, during formal events such as musical concerts, poetry readings, award ceremonies, and banquets, especially when an African-American is a featured orator, applaud and extend standing ovations so frequently to the point that even insignificant utterance receives accolades?

48. ***Community Environment-Why is it that*** most of the interviewees expressed that most male persons of the African-American Persuasion who happen to be pop or rap music artists wear baggy and sagging pants, full leather jackets when performing (regardless of the seasons), don a diamond accent necklace, silver, gold, or platinum medallion, multiple carat diamond earrings, and headbands? Their attire is primarily the same and lacks individuality.

49. ***Community Environment-Why is it that*** most of the interviewees expressed that most male persons of the Caucasian Persuasion who happen to be country western music artists wear tightly fitted denim jeans accompanied by a one to two-inch-wide belt with an embossed belt buckle, cowboy hat, plaid shirt, and cowboy boots? Their attire is primarily the same and lacks individuality.

50. ***Community Environment-Why is it that*** most of the interviewees expressed that most persons of the Caucasian Persuasion seem to have no sense of personal space distance? When conversing with others, most male persons of the Caucasian Persuasion have a tendency to position themselves within one foot to two feet from the person whom they are addressing. Most African-Americans are more comfortable

with, and usually are separated by, at least two to three feet of personal space distance while conversing.

51. *Community Environment-Why is it that* most of the interviewees expressed that most persons of the Caucasian Persuasion are more prone to commit suicide than persons of the African-American Persuasion when life issues multiple challenges or circumstances one may judge insurmountable?

52. *Community Environment-Why is it that* most of the interviewees expressed that most persons of the African-American Persuasion believe that persons of the Caucasian Persuasion are historically initiators of domestic terrorism in America especially against them and other ethnic groups? By controlling all major industries, corporations, financial institutions, and directing all governmental affairs, domestic terrorist initiatives were well funded to advance the cause.

53. *Community Environment-Why is it that* most of the interviewees expressed that most persons of the Caucasian Persuasion who are impressed with an African-American that communicates well, clearly and consistently exclaim that "they are very articulate," but rarely express the same adulation about persons of the Caucasian Persuasion?

54. *Community Environment-Why is it that* most of the interviewees expressed that most male persons of the African-American Persuasion lick/wet their lips consistently when being interviewed via television broadcasting?

55. *Community Environment-Why is it that* most of the interviewees expressed that persons of the Caucasian Persuasion generalize and label any male person of the African-American Persuasion who expresses his opinion about African-American interests as the African-American spokesperson, voice of the

community, or community leader? Such a title is rarely, if ever, placed on any male person of the Caucasian Persuasion when expressing the interests of his community.

56. ***Community Environment-Why is it that*** persons of the Caucasian Persuasion have no qualms about their actions to abruptly move from a major city to the surrounding suburbs (White flight) to remove themselves from what they deem moral and economic decay, (i.e., African-American mayoral leadership, city council/alderman/borough leadership, ad valorem taxes, crime, the public school system, and traffic)? But, on the other hand, they make their living within the city or community from which they commute daily. Additionally, they complain about ad valorem taxes being increased, narrow roads, lack of traffic lights, lack of fire protection services, and basic public services in their new locations. They also demand that all of the issues mentioned above be addressed and corrected to accommodate their needs. Is this a clear example of such outlooks as, "I want to have my cake and to eat it too" and "Damn it, I worked hard for it, and I deserve it"?

57. ***Community Environment-Why is it that*** most of the interviewees expressed that male persons of the African-American Persuasion lack respect for females, especially those who are heavily entrenched in the hip-hop or rap scene, by calling female persons of the African-American Persuasion bitches, stank hoes, hood rats, chicken heads, shorties, ghetto queens, skanks, and other demeaning designations? Whereas, male persons of the Caucasian Persuasion rarely and certainly do not televise or publicly express their ill thoughts for or address female persons of the Caucasian Persuasion in such a debasing manner.

58. ***Community Environment-Why is it that*** most of the interviewees expressed that most female persons of the

African-American Persuasion allow male persons of any persuasion entrenched in the hip-hop or rap scene to address them in demeaning, derogatory, and disrespectful ways?

59. *Community Environment-Why is it that* most of the interviewees expressed that most female persons of the African-American Persuasion, when dining in a group, seldom tip waiters and waitresses or find it difficult to provide a gratuity of 20% or more?

60. *Community Environment-Why is it that* most of the interviewees expressed that persons of the African-American Persuasion when discussing persons of the Caucasian Persuasion while speaking in a normal tone immediately secure a lower decibel by whispering or muffling the word "White" when describing the ethnicity of said group? This act is not only done in a mixed ethnic setting, but even in rooms or places where all persons are of the African-American Persuasion.

61. *Community Environment-Why is it that* nearly all of the interviewees expressed that most male persons of the African-American Persuasion primarily between eighteen to fifty years of age, when approaching a traffic light and reducing car speed to come to a complete stop, they have to see who is in the adjacent car? If they are in an extreme reclining position, they will sit up for the exclusive purpose to catch a view of the adjacent car driver and passenger(s). Whereas, most male persons of the Caucasian Persuasion hardly ever adjust their straight forward position when at a complete stop waiting for a traffic light change.

62. *Community Environment-Why is it that* nearly all of the interviewees expressed that most male persons of the Caucasian Persuasion who have a thirst for beer purchase a full six pack more often than purchasing a single 40-ounce, two regular

12-ounces, or any combination shy of a six pack? Conversely, most male persons of the African-American Persuasion purchase single beers more often in lieu of purchasing a full six pack.

63. ***Community Environment-Why is it that*** nearly all of the interviewees expressed that most male and female persons of the African-American Persuasion who participate in high school, college, or hometown parade marching bands, drill teams, dance groups, etc., are expected and compelled to shake, dangle, snatch, pop, stroke, grind their bodies, and other physically provocative moves to arouse the crowd? The absence of such performance among most African-American spectators would be extremely disappointing and critical. Surprisingly, even young ladies under twelve years of age are allowed and celebrated to perform provocatively.

64. ***Community Environment-Why is it that*** local and national media groups are so predictable when carrying out an assignment or report on a live scene in African-American communities; they seek out the most physically and mentally challenged and uneducated African-American to serve as their first-hand witness? The interviewer aggressively accentuates the abundance of ignorance the interviewee possesses. Rarely do the media seek out or interview persons of the Caucasian Persuasion that have parallel challenges.

65. ***Community Environment-Why is it that*** nearly all of the interviewees believed that most male law enforcement officers of the Caucasian Persuasion are more inclined to exercise excessive physical restraint practices and the use of excessive force on persons of the African-American Persuasion? However, male persons of the African-American Persuasion are seldom cited for excessive physical restraint practices and

excessive force against persons of the Caucasian Persuasion, regardless of their resistance or physical aggression.

66. *Community Environment-Why is it that* nearly all of the interviewees expressed that most persons of the Caucasian Persuasion abhor the results of African-Americans use of the legal system that unfolds in their favor even if they were clearly innocent?

67. *Community Environment-Why is it that* nearly all of the interviewees expressed that most persons of the Caucasian Persuasion publicly label persons of the African-American Persuasion "as animals" and "monsters" when an alleged crime has been committed by an African-American against a person of the Caucasian Persuasion? Why is it that the predetermined guilty verdict is never mentally removed when a "jury of their peers" finds them unequivocally not guilty?

68. *Community Environment-Why is it that* nearly all of the interviewees expressed that most male persons of the Caucasian Persuasion expel gas in public settings with the absence of a hint of embarrassment more often than male persons of the African-American Persuasion, who are still labeled as ill-mannered and repulsive?

69. *Community Environment-Why is it that* nearly all of the interviewees expressed that persons of the Caucasian Persuasion are persistent in written communications expressing that all fictional heroes, noteworthy inventors, spiritual authors, great philosophers, science researchers, medical experts or any profession, or professionals who have contributed to society significantly are all recognized and assumed as being of the Caucasian Persuasion?

Speak It My Friend. You Are So Observant!

70. ***Community Environment-Why is it that*** nearly all of the interviewees of both persuasions expressed that in most weddings of persons of the African-American Persuasion, the bride does not consider the importance of dress design patterns for the female wedding participants? In most cases, the design pattern does not complement all persons and sizes? A size 4-6 close-fitting pattern is not necessarily flattering for a person that wears a size 24-26 and vice-versa.

71. ***Community Environment-Why is it that*** nearly all of the interviewees expressed that most persons of the Caucasian Persuasion as early as twelve years of age to sixty-five are encouraged to save money and purchase their needs first and then their wants second? Why is it that saving money and less spending are not compelling objectives in the African-American community?

72. ***Community Environment-Why is it that*** nearly all of the interviewees expressed that most persons of the Caucasian Persuasion tend to seek immediate resolutions to physical imperfections, (i.e., liposuction, intestinal reductions, nose restructuring, eyelid restructuring, facial cheek bone restructuring, breast implants, leg calves implants, penis implants, pectoral implants, hip reductions, buttock implants, etc.), more so than persons of the African-American Persuasion? Why is vanity deemed the top determinant of physical and social acceptance? But if an African-American publicly exclaims the notion of seeking physical surgical enhancements, most persons of the Caucasian Persuasion categorize them as pathetic or lazy.

73. ***Community Environment-Why is it that*** nearly all of the interviewees expressed that most persons of the Caucasian

Persuasion exert every effort to justify cheating to receive office promotions, physical improvements, physical enhancement medication, racial/ethnic preferences, sexual escapades, etc., regardless of the circumstance? But if persons of the African-American Persuasion indulge in said actions, they will be publicly demeaned and discredited. People will viciously abhor their existence and vigilantly pursue opportunities to humiliate them publicly.

74. *Community Environment-Why is it that* nearly all of the interviewees expressed that, in most weddings of persons of the African-American Persuasion guests' participation during the reception dinner is always delayed by one to two hours? The guests in most instances have to wait for the wedding party to arrive after their photo session, whereas, during weddings of mostly persons of the Caucasian Persuasion, the guests arc usually invited to partake and proceed with the reception dinner within thirty to forty minutes.

75. *Community Environment-Why is it that* nearly all of the interviewees expressed that most persons of the African-American Persuasion are considered strong, resourceful, and survivors under any circumstance with the absence of contemplating suicide? However, most persons of the Caucasian Persuasion are considered not as strong or resourceful, nor as survivors, especially when life issues financial circumstances that are extremely challenging.

76. *Community Environment-Why is it that* nearly all of the interviewees expressed that most male persons of the African-American Persuasion between the ages of 16-25 are considered weak when they are so quick and prefer the use of deadly force (guns) when confronted with what one would consider diminutive differences? Any form of an altercation, especially among two African-American males, can result in a handgun

discharge. Why does the same group of African-American males exercise learned behavior to eliminate the opposition by resorting to firearm exchange whenever a circumstance presents itself? Why is it that the group mentioned above is deemed weak, cowardly, and outright ignorant as expressed by many mature African-American males? This group of young African-American males projects the image of "walking hard, looking hard, and talking hard," but is extremely fragile. Are such acts among young African-American males a continuation of the Willie Lynch theory? Where is the strength of the mature African-American male in mitigating the displaced fear and anger of the young African-American male?

77. ***Community Environment-Why is it that*** nearly all of the interviewees expressed that most male persons of the Caucasian Persuasion feverishly value the expression, "never kick a man when he's down," but ruthlessly exhibit actions that convey a different philosophy that loudly exclaims, "can you think of a better time?" Does this conduct equate the notion, "always take advantage of the feeble and less fortunate" and use laws introduced and written mostly for and by persons of the Caucasians Persuasion to justify these actions?

78. ***Community Environment-Why is it that*** nearly all of the interviewees expressed that most persons of the African-American Persuasion, who are clearly categorized socio-economically as lower middle class via U.S. census, purchase or lease vehicles (Cadillac Escalade, 430 Lexus, all series of Jaguars, all series of Mercedes, and all series of BMWs) that are equivalent to or exceed their net worth or the total value of their residence? These purchases in most cases have payments (36 to 72 months) that represent approximately 25% to 50% of their monthly take-home income.

79.   ***Community Environment-Why is it that*** nearly all of the interviewees expressed that in most African-American communities where crime is prevalent but contained, local, state, and congressional leadership fundamentally lack aggression to combat the criminal forces? They appear to condone continued acts of violence until they bleed into majority Caucasian communities, and only then does it becomes a "major issue" and "national crisis."

80.   ***Community Environment-Why is it that*** nearly all of the interviewees expressed that most persons of the Caucasian Persuasion do not name their female offspring with names that end with an "a," or males names that end with an "a" or "ous," have a French pronunciation, and are complicated to spell? Take, for example, female name as Shauda, Varesia, Shaniqua, Shaneka, Damekia, Swauvaya, Chellsia, Marquitia, Shandrea, Breannia, and male names as Octavious, La'Quarious, Kavarious, DeMarious, etc.

81.   ***Community Environment-Why is it that*** nearly all of the interviewees expressed that most persons of the African-American Persuasion do not name their female offspring Mary Beth, Ashley Ann, Becky Elizabeth, Elizabeth Ann, Patsy Leigh, Charlie Susan or Barbie Sue?

82.   ***Community Environment-Why is it that*** nearly all of the interviewees expressed that young male persons of the African-American Persuasion wear du-rags solely or underneath a baseball cap, two undershirts massed by a dry cleaned/starched shirt, a pair of boxer brief underwear or compression shorts, and gym shorts underneath oversized thick denim jeans in 95° to 100° summer heat? This attire ensemble is usually multi-seasonal. One has difficulty discerning the logic of this attire.

83. ***Community Environment-Why is it that*** nearly all of the interviewees expressed that most persons of the African-American Persuasion who are lower to middle class have the distinct and common urge to barbecue and entertain guests on their front porch, carport or front lawn when they have sizable and perfectly manicured back yards?

84. ***Community Environment-Why is it that*** nearly all of the interviewees expressed that when most persons of the African-American Persuasion are invited to a business party, they are more concerned about what's on the menu in lieu of being interested in the list of invited guests and a method in which to take advantage of business networking opportunities?

85. ***Community Environment-Why is it that*** most of the interviewees expressed that young male persons of the African-American Persuasion commonly use the most degrading and derogatory word, "Nigger/Nigga," in addressing and meeting other male persons of the African-America Persuasion, and that it has no impact on the historical use of the word as spoken to African-Americans by persons of the Caucasian Persuasion? African-Americans shout the use of this word proudly as a "gesture of endearment" in the presence of persons of the Caucasian Persuasion. But, why is it forbidden for a person of the Caucasian Persuasion to utter the word, "Nigger/Nigga," without the threat of potential physical abuse or being labeled a racist?

86. ***Community Environment-Why is it that*** there consistently appears to be more persons of the African-American Persuasion who frequent traffic court than persons of the Caucasian Persuasion? During these visits (approximately 1,000 per week in cities with a population of 400,000), the average person of the African-American Persuasion pays $150.00 for the citation plus court costs, while most persons of the Caucasian Persuasion

contend that African-Americans do not contribute directly or indirectly to the city's economy. Although African-Americans contributions are unfortunate and costly for alleged violators, is said assertion debunked?

87. ***Community Environment-Why is it that*** nearly all of the interviewees expressed that most persons of the African-American Persuasion believe that Affirmative Action is the best approach to addressing and removing employment disparities? They also believe that it will provide equal opportunities and level playing fields for them when they are usually not in a power position to make final employment hiring decisions. African-Americans make up a very small percentage of presidents, CEOs, CFOs, and COOs of major corporations. The interviewees believe that African-Americans who are granted opportunities for employment through Affirmative Action, are monitored excessively, reminded daily that they are the "token," and will be ridiculed severely with statements that precede their employment demise such as "just wait; it's not if they screw up, but when they screw up, they are out of here."

88. ***Community Environment-Why is it that*** at most older Southern country clubs where the majority of members are males of the Caucasian Persuasion, rarely are there older staff/workers that happen to be of the same ethnic persuasion? Most country clubs usually have young male staff or interns of the Caucasian Persuasion. It is very uncommon to employ young male staff or intern persons of the African-American Persuasion, but they most often and consistently have senior male staff/workers of the African-American Persuasion. Additionally, the Caucasian male country club members never address the senior African-American male staff workers by their surname. They are addressed without exception by their first name, seconds away from addressing them as "boy."

89. ***Community Environment-Why is it that*** nearly all of the interviewees expressed that young African-American males should restrain from car cruising, "four deep" late nights, knowing that they may be subjected to being profiled and stopped by law officers? Once pulled over, the officer may intentionally or inadvertently provoke the African-American male driver or passengers. Then tempers flare, the officer concludes his or her "life is at risk or threatened" and the simple traffic infraction spirals to an avoidable deadly tragedy. This calculated move by, more often than not, a Caucasian male enforcement officer compels the driver or passengers to react defensively. The officer, in turn, responds forcefully and invites the justification to employ deadly force even though a large percent of African-American males who have been in said circumstance, unquestionably are innocent and unarmed.

90. ***Community Environment-Why is it that*** nearly all of the interviewees expressed that most persons of the African-American Persuasion spend a large percentage of money on material items or items that do not appreciate in value annually, dissimilar to persons of the Caucasian Persuasion? Most African-American females spend excessive amounts of money on hair designs, hair products, nails, shoes, clothes, and purses. Most African-American males spend excessive amounts of money on tailored shirts, clothes, dress shoes, basketball sneakers, dry cleaning, jewelry, cars, and car rims.

91. ***Community Environment-Why is it that*** nearly all of the interviewees expressed that most persons of the African-American Persuasion rarely invest their money in services or products that yield an average of six to twelve percent interest and appreciate in value over a ten year period?

92. ***Community Environment-Why is it that*** nearly all of the interviewees expressed that most persons of the Caucasian

Persuasion have more physical ailments during working hours and create excuses to request time off from work, but criticize legitimate requests persons of the African-American Persuasion submit?

93. *Community Environment-Why is it that* nearly all of the interviewees expressed that most persons of the Caucasian Persuasion who own pet dogs or cats have an incredible urge to frequently "French kiss" their pets? They are constantly kissing on them or allowing the pet to lick them in and on the mouth.

94. *Community Environment-Why is it that* nearly all of the interviewees expressed that most persons of the Caucasian Persuasion who live off the spoils of past government legislation which allowed them to advance financially for multiple generations believe persons of the African-American Persuasion arc not savvy enough, haven't worked as hard, or do not have the wit to acquire wealth as they have?

95. *Community Environment-Why is it that* nearly all of the interviewees expressed that when most persons of the Caucasian Persuasion file a lawsuit that includes punitive damages, they are considered brilliant for using the legal system to gain financial relief and seek deserved justice? However, when persons of the African-American Persuasion file a lawsuit for punitive damages, they are immediately deemed lazy and get-over artists, or that "they always want something for nothing."

96. *Community Environment-Why is it that* nearly all of the interviewees expressed that most persons of the Caucasian Persuasion who make the same income and have a similar credit score as that of persons of the African-American Persuasion are able to purchase a home that is worth at least $250,000.00 or more with significant ease, (i.e., less collateral, lower interest

rate, interest points, etc), than that of persons of the African-American Persuasion?

97. ***Community Environment-Why is it that*** nearly all of the interviewees expressed that persons of the African-American Persuasion rarely adopt or render foster care to children of the Caucasian Persuasion, but persons of the Caucasian Persuasion frequently adopt and provide foster care to children of the African-American Persuasion?

98. ***Community Environment-Why is it that*** nearly all of the interviewees expressed that most persons of the African-American Persuasion have never been taught how to invest their earnings (real estate, futures, options, mutual funds, stock, bonds, etc.) to yield the greatest return on their investment?

99. ***Community Environment-Why is it that*** most of the interviewees expressed that most male persons of the Caucasian Persuasion have immense difficulty understanding the concept of affirmative action? They express and project the belief that all persons of the African-American Persuasion hired through this initiative prevented a Caucasian from gaining employment. They contend that Caucasians worked harder and earned their way, but the standards are always lowered to include persons of the African-American Persuasion in the workforce. If one isolated ill-fated incident arises that happened to involve a person of the African-American Persuasion who experienced the Affirmative Action employment initiative, the entire program has failed, and all African-Americans should be happy that they have a job because they were not qualified from day one; they were only hired to meet a quota. They are never hired because of their hard work but only and absolutely because they are African-Americans. Is the inference that all persons of the Caucasian Persuasion deserve to have only the best of opportunities regardless of their intellect, and all

African-Americans should be happy to have a job (less pay/ lower management only) regardless of their hard work and intellect or that they are more deserving of being street peddlers or worthless subordinates?

100. ***Community Environment-Why is it that*** most of the interviewees expressed that most persons of the Caucasian Persuasion contend that if an African-American graduate Magna Cum Laude in physics, biophysics, nuclear physics, chemistry, aerospace engineering, medicine, law, architecture, mathematics or education from a Historically Black College or University, their accomplishments are deemed substandard? However, if that same African-American received the same academic honors from a majority college or university, he/she was simply a pass through or accepted only because he/she was African-Americans/met a quota. They are convinced that there had to have been a person of the Caucasian Persuasion, who worked harder but got looked over or bumped just to allow a person of the African-American Persuasion to advance.

101. ***Community Environment-Why is it that*** most of the interviewees expressed that most persons of the Caucasian Persuasion refuse to believe that they are beneficiaries of the best employment and business opportunities simply because they are of the Caucasian Persuasion? Why is it that most persons of the African-American Persuasion believe that the abovementioned communication has substantial validity because of the coined phrase commonly expressed, "it's who you know as opposed to what you know" that affects many hiring results.

102. ***Community Environment-Why is it that*** most of the interviewees expressed that most persons of the Caucasian Persuasion believe that proliferations of addictive drugs were cultivated, harvested, and abound in African-American

communities? Why is it that they also believe that African-Americans established and structured drug distribution territories, embraced the joys of poor housing, poor education, joblessness, the perpetuation of daily violence, and maintained that persons of the Caucasian Persuasion were not a party to any of the above-depraved acts? Moreover, expressions, such as the following are frequently voiced: "Why can't most of them work hard and go to college to better themselves?" "We worked hard to realize our American dream, why can't they?"

103. *Community Environment-Why is it that* most of the interviewees expressed that the legs of most young male persons of the Caucasian Persuasion, from their knee caps to their feet, show few battle scars, (i.e., cuts, remnants of surgical stitching, chicken pox, mosquito bites or abrasion), whereas the legs of most young male persons of the African-American Persuasion show numerous battle scars?

104. *Community Environment-Why is it that* most of the interviewees expressed that most male persons of the African-American Persuasion who own what is considered an expensive and luxurious vehicle drive in cities, especially Southern ones, with their windows down in 80° to 100° summer heat? Why not use the air conditioning system when the vehicle's interior and exterior temperature can be deemed unbearable?

105. *Community Environment-Why is it that* most of the interviewees expressed that most persons of the African-American Persuasion do not hold their children accountable when they are knowledgeable of the fact that their children pitch rocks and bricks at abandoned buildings in their communities in an attempt to shatter the storefront facade glazing? Does this add to the depreciation of property value in their communities?

106. ***Community Environment-Why is it that*** most of the interviewees expressed that most persons of the African-American Persuasion feel that they are compelled to shoulder the burden of all African-Americans when another person of the same ethnicity displays their ignorance, stupidity, and moronic qualities in public settings?

107. ***Community Environment-Why is it that*** most of the interviewees believe that most household products are designed for the female persons of the Caucasian Persuasion drastically to reduce their basic household workload or chores and perpetuate progressive laziness? Were these products introduced when the Caucasian "Miss Anne" could no longer afford the domestic labor of African-American women?

108. ***Community Environment-Why is it that*** most of the interviewees expressed that in most sexual assault cases when male persons of the African-American Persuasion are accused of assaulting female persons of the Caucasian Persuasion, they receive brutal criticism and are labeled as sex crazed brutes and menaces to society? Local and national media charge them with a guilty verdict until proven innocent, and they are more likely to receive longer prison sentences than male persons of the Caucasian Persuasion that are accused of sexual aggressions towards female persons of the African-American Persuasion?

109. ***Community Environment-Why is it that*** most of the interviewees expressed that the female of the Caucasian Persuasion is considered to be the most powerful and dangerous beings in present day culture when male aggression or physical threats of any persuasion is made toward them? This torch of power has been carried and exercised profoundly, chiefly in expressed communications of accusations of male sexual assaults with the absence of witnesses or evidence to substantiate the charges. Do female persons of the African-American

Persuasion receive the same attention? Same gender. Same circumstance. Different response.

110. ***Community Environment-Why is it that*** most of the interviewees expressed that most female persons of the Caucasian Persuasion can make sexual assault and physical threat accusations at any time, any place, and against any male person of the African-American Persuasion, and most persons of the Caucasian Persuasion will not question their veracity but vehemently and feverishly champion their pursuit of the assailant?

111. ***Community Environment-Why is it that*** most of the interviewees expressed that in most lower-class African-American communities, multiple cars are parked in front of their homes on the front lawn in lieu of their driveways?

112. ***Community Environment-Why is it that*** most of the interviewees expressed that most affluent persons of both the African-American and Caucasian Persuasions group all lower-middle-class African-Americans with persons of the Caucasian Persuasion that are labeled "Po White Trash" (PWT) when discussing socioeconomic issues? This grouping of African-Americans and PWT is commonly expressed in the most unpleasing and demeaning fashion. Are there different economic and social classes for all people as determined by the U.S. Census Bureau?

113. ***Community Environment-Why is it that*** most of the interviewees expressed that most persons of the African-American Persuasion believe that southern females of the Caucasian Persuasion are not as spiritually grounded as they would like you to believe when they attend church every day of the week praising the Lord and denouncing societal ills, but they will proudly attend a public beating or execution of an

African-American male at a moment's notice with a sense of euphoria?

114. ***Community Environment-Why is it that*** most of the interviewees expressed that most female persons of the African-American Persuasion are more prone to don a massive diamond cluster wedding ring in lieu of a simple half, one or two karat diamond solitaire? Is quality a factor in the selection or the ring diameter?

115. ***Community Environment-Why is it that*** most of the interviewees expressed that most female persons of the Caucasian Persuasion between the ages of 21 to 35 years old are more inclined to select beer as their beverage of choice and drink from a bottle at parties, restaurants or nightclubs more often than female persons of the African-American Persuasion?

116. ***Community Environment-Why is it that*** most of the interviewees expressed that when a pastor of the Caucasian Persuasion who has a weekly worship service, the initial congregation is approximately 50% African-Americans and 50% Caucasians, eventually experience a shift in ethnic demographics to approximately 75% African-Americans and 25% Caucasians? Rarely has the opposite demographic shift ever taken place. Why do Caucasians leave church even if the pastor is a dynamic orator and a teacher of the Word and 85% of the church officers are persons of Caucasian Persuasion? Is this the Christian mindset of "separate shall remain separate" or when every circumstance without question is in their favor?

117. ***Community Environment-Why is it that*** most of the interviewees expressed that male persons of the African-American Persuasion between the ages of 13 to 35 rarely if ever change their attire to appropriate clothing, (i.e., swim trunks long or short) when attending pool parties or beach functions?

Why do they consistently don baggy pants, extra large/long tee shirts, oversized caps with or without a du-rag, etc.?

118. ***Community Environment-Why is it that*** most of the interviewees expressed that most "Action Heroes" as depicted on network television and in the printed press are 99.99% of the Caucasian Persuasion? Is this by design or just happenstance? Are there African-American cartoonists or do both African-Americans and Caucasians find African-American Action Heroes unappealing and unmarketable?

119. ***Community Environment-Why is it that*** most of the interviewees expressed that most persons of the African-American Persuasion vigorously aspire to purchase homes or property in upscale predominantly Caucasian neighborhood developments instead of upscale predominantly African-American neighborhoods? The interviewees also noted that persons of the Caucasian Persuasion rarely exhibit little interest in residing in upscale predominantly African-American neighborhood developments?

120. ***Community Environment-Why is it that*** most of the interviewees expressed that most male persons of the Caucasian Persuasion who are thirty years of age or older do not equip their cars with what is commonly termed "dubs" or "spinners?" However, most male persons of the African-American Persuasion within the same age group are more inclined to equip their cars with expensive after-market faddish accessories such as silver door trimming, low profile tires, non-manufactured dark tinted windows, front grills, underside lighting, expensive rims, etc.

121. ***Community Environment-Why is it that*** most of the interviewees expressed that most persons of the Caucasian Persuasion rarely shout or hiss in worship services as a means

to express their spiritual emotions? It is commonplace for older generations of the African-American Persuasion to do so in multiple forms.

122. ***Community Environment-Why is it that*** most of the interviewees expressed that most persons of the Caucasian Persuasion are more inclined to allow their toddler to take pleasure in having a pacifier at the age of four and older more so than persons of the African-American Persuasion?

123. ***Community Environment-Why is it that*** most of the interviewees expressed that in most lower to middle-income African-American communities retail shopping centers and convenient neighborhood stores parking lots are blanketed with fast food trash bags, bottles, cups, cans, diapers, and other debris that appear to be commonplace? Conversely, little debris is found in lower to middle-income Caucasian communities retail shopping centers parking lots and convenient neighborhood stores parking lots.

124. ***Community Environment-Why is it that*** most of the interviewees expressed that when most gospel artists who are of the African-American Persuasion reach the chorus phase of a song, they begin to yell and scream with emotions to the point that the words are difficult to understand and recognize? This similar act is performed by hard rock artists that happen to be of the Caucasian Persuasion but is done throughout the entire song.

125. ***Community Environment-Why is it that*** most of the interviewees expressed that most persons of the Caucasian Persuasion rarely display African-American sculptures, paintings, portraits, or any artwork in their place of business or homes whereas, most persons of the African-American Persuasion display artwork, paintings, portraits, and sculptures,

designed and created by persons of the Caucasian Persuasion in their places of business as well as in their homes?

126. ***Community Environment-Why is it that*** most of the interviewees expressed that most reality shows feature persons of the Caucasian Persuasion by an estimated low of 5 to 1 and a high of 10 to 1 to every person of the African-American Persuasion, especially when a winning purse is a part of the equation? Thus, the chances for an African-American winning the grand purse are considerably low.

127. ***Community Environment-Why is it that*** most of the interviewees expressed that most persons of the Caucasian Persuasion believe that if an African-American wins the purse on cable or major network reality shows, ratings will plummet? Thus, a showing of African-American participation is only a ploy to thwart public ethnic criticism.

128. ***Community Environment-Why is it that*** most of the interviewees expressed that most persons of the African-American Persuasion believe that cable or major network reality shows did not or will never provide equal diversity on shows such as The Real World, Road Rules, The Apprentice, The Bachelor, Big Brother, Survivor, Million Dollar Listing, The Contender, The Amazing Race, Dancing with the Stars, The Voice, Top Chef, Naked and Afraid, Shark Tank, The Billionaire, Kept, etc., just to name a few? Interviewees continued to express, that the shows as mentioned above usually had or have a limit of one to two African-American hosts or contenders at a time.

129. ***Community Environment-Why is it that*** the majority of the interviewees expressed that most persons of the African-American and Caucasian Persuasions have a tendency to congregate with each perspective ethnic group when

participating in large, diverse group functions in lieu of conversing and gathering for any significant time with the opposite ethnic group?

130. *Community Environment-Why is it that* the majority of the interviewees expressed that most persons of the Caucasian Persuasion address their grandparents as "Paw Paw, Granddad, Grandpop, Mam-maw, Grandfather, Grandmama, Nana, and Memaw" and most persons of the African-American Persuasion address their grandparents as "Big Mama, Big Daddy, Gramps, Grandma, and Madea?"

131. *Community Environment-Why is it that* the majority of the interviewees expressed that most persons of the Caucasian Persuasion assume that all persons of the African-American Persuasion know each other?

132. *Community Environment-Why is it that* the majority of the interviewees expressed that most persons of the Caucasian Persuasion assume that they have to communicate in the hip-hop vernacular to feel as though they can fit in or be accepted by persons of the African-American Persuasion?

133. *Community Environment-Why is it that* the majority of the interviewees expressed that most male persons of the Caucasian Persuasion who fall in the lower to the middle-class socioeconomic bracket are more inclined to own multiple guns, assault or military grade rifles, and ammunition than male persons of the African-American Persuasion in the same socioeconomic bracket?

134. *Community Environment-Why is it that* the majority of the interviewees expressed that most children of the Caucasian Persuasion are more apt to read a book than to watch multiple hours of television? Conversely, most children of

the African-American Persuasion are more inclined to watch multiple hours (at least thirty hours weekly) of television in lieu of reading a book. Is African-American parenting responsible for this disparity?

135. ***Community Environment-Why is it that*** the majority of the interviewees expressed that most male rap artists of the African-American Persuasion do not express or display nearly the level of intense anger during a public performance that was once quite common several years ago? The lifelong anger facial expressions and body language have been replaced with more pleasant facial gestures. Did the industry change them or was it a façade to display hardiness to be accepted?

Check This Out.

136. ***Community Environment-Why is it that*** the majority of the interviewees expressed that most male persons of the African-American Persuasion rarely express interest in hiking, hunting, camping or white water rafting with their families, friends or colleagues? Conversely, most male persons of the Caucasian Persuasion are more inclined to indulge in these adventures.

137. ***Community Environment-Why is it that*** the majority of the interviewees expressed that most persons of the Caucasian Persuasion are more inclined to prop their bare feet on the dashboard of a vehicle as a gesture of relaxation when traveling distances beyond the city or town in which they live more so than persons of the African-American Persuasion?

138. ***Community Environment-Why is it that*** the majority of the interviewees expressed that most hair salons in the African-American community over-book their clients to the point that the client has to wait two to three hours before being served?

Additionally, the hair stylists rarely voice their apologies or show any concern for the delay.

139. ***Community Environment-Why is it that*** the abduction or alleged homicide of a female person of the Caucasian Persuasion is subject to receive considerable, intense, and sustained national news coverage more so than female persons of the African-American Persuasion who have experienced a similar horrendous attack? Is the value of life for both ethnic groups the same or is one less than the other?

140. ***Community Environment-Why is it that*** the majority of the interviewees expressed that most male persons of the African-American Persuasion believe that approximately 1/3 of all African-American males are incarcerated? They also believe that those who are incarcerated were convicted of much lesser crimes than that of male persons of the Caucasian Persuasion. Further, they believe that judicial actions are designed to widen methodically the two ethnic group's economic disparities which continue to plague the capitalistic veins of this country.

141. ***Community Environment-Why is it that*** the majority of the interviewees expressed that most persons of the African-American Persuasion believe that the Caucasian female does not have an excuse for being financially distressed? They believe society has and will continue to yield to their every need, desire, and victimization. Additionally, societal reactions have suggested that the Caucasian female is top priority when bringing an alleged aggressor against her to justice swiftly with significant and unparalleled comparison to that of the African-American female.

142. ***Community Environment-Why is it that*** the majority of the interviewees expressed that most persons of the Caucasian Persuasion rarely say "excuse me" when trying to pass an

African-American in aisles of convenient stores, shopping malls, and similar establishments? Instead of kindly offering an "excuse me," they will stand quietly expecting the person of a different ethnic background to acknowledge them and permit clearance for them.

143. Community Environment-Why is it that the majority of the interviewees expressed that most businesspersons, educators, politicians, and other community male leaders of the African-American Persuasion do not challenge each other to mentor at least two to three young adult African-American males? Most of the above potential mentors are aware of the African-American youth statistics of fatherless homes, receiving an incomplete education, and the high risk of possible incarceration, but most still seem to accept the complete loss of a generation.

144. Community Environment-Why is it that the majority of the interviewees expressed that most male persons of the Caucasian Persuasion encourage and/or demand the incarceration of young African-American males, "young thugs," regardless of the charge, but are outraged that their tax dollars pay approximately $35,000 to $60,000 in tax funds per year per inmate's incarceration?

145. Community Environment-Why is it that the majority of the interviewees expressed that most male African-American rap artists have substantially reduced their crouch grabbing, excessive invective language, and thug mentality projections (facial frowns, short verbal communication, and hard façade) in the past five years? Did money, primetime audiences, understanding marketability, or the exhaustion of the acts compel them to change?

146. Community Environment-Why is it that the majority of the interviewees expressed that most older and mature

African-American males define today's hip-hop "young thugs" as weak, perpetrators, lost, and girly men when they resort to lethal violence over the most minute issues? Additionally, older and mature African-American males believe that young men who tote guns as a dismal form of intimidation are the weakest link in the chain of all African-American males.

147. ***Community Environment-Why is it that*** the majority of the interviewees expressed that most older and mature African-American males believe that if younger African-American males would refrain from trying to prove themselves as "hard" or "thugs" and choose their battles in lieu of fighting over every matter and/or reacting to every gesture of opposition, most prisons would be half empty and more lives would be saved? They also believe good parenting, mentoring, guidance, education, and employment opportunities are still the solutions to reducing violence in their communities.

148. ***Community Environment-Why is it that*** the majority of the interviewees expressed that most African-American males are not responding to the inner needs and feelings expressed by today's hip-hop "young thugs" that they want real mentoring, (i.e., a male figure to show them that they care, one that really loves them, establishing moral boundaries, and providing structure)? They also have expressed that their fathers do not necessarily have to live in the home or have daily contact, but they ask for their fathers or mentors to be consistent, truthful, show up, provide guidance, extend praises, tell them that they are loved, and more importantly, show them how to be responsible, and productive

149. ***Community Environment-Why is it that*** the majority of the interviewees expressed that most persons of the Caucasian Persuasion believe that the lack of education, job opportunities, property ownership, business, and circulation of money are

the culprits of the deterioration of any community, especially the African-American community? Most Caucasians are convinced that job opportunities are abundant; everybody is operating and playing on a level playing field. It is further noted, that most persons of the Caucasian Persuasion believe that a large portion of African-Americans simply choose not to work and rather bask in the diffused rays of poverty. Some believe the lack of opportunities in African-American communities is unequivocally and solely their problem.

150. ***Community Environment-Why is it that*** the majority of the interviewees expressed that most male persons of the African-American Persuasion who work with committed focus, due diligence, and who possess infinite wisdom in their line of work find it difficult to fathom the idea of creating business opportunities for themselves for fear that persons of both the African-American and Caucasian Persuasions will not support their businesses? The most frequent statement expressed regarding their future outlook is as follows: "working for someone is your place in society if you wish to live semi-comfortably."

151. ***Community Environment-Why is it that*** the majority of the interviewees expressed that male persons of the Caucasian Persuasion are more prone to exercise polygamy in the United States? All realms of the media rarely report African-American males exercising polygamy.

152. ***Community Environment-Why is it that*** the majority of the interviewees expressed that persons of the Caucasian Persuasion are privileged in all fields of entrepreneurial ventures and the business industry? Additionally, most persons of the Caucasian Persuasion believe persons of the African-American Persuasion unquestionably and inexcusably have equal opportunities to secure the same. Pigmentation is not an excuse. Moreover, persons of the Caucasian Persuasion believe African-Americans have dominated the music and sports industries. However, most persons of the Caucasian Persuasion fully comprehend that they are the controlling entities in both industries, and that equates power and wealth. Thus, observation facilitates truth that persons of the Caucasian Persuasion by design control the following industries: banking, construction, medical, sports, music, automotive, educational, transportation, literary, gaming, hospitality, manufacturing, petroleum, chemical, aerospace, sales, fashion, media, etc. Do African-Americans really have a chance? Why are African-Americans economic advancements feared, purposely limited, and definitively controlled? Is control the daily charge to sustain positional and financial superiority?

153. *Community Environment-Why is it that* the majority of the interviewees expressed that the majority of both Caucasian and African-American Masons do not recognize each other or have joint memberships and visitation authority? Each has separate memberships and visitation authority but share similar philosophies, (i.e., African-American males are associated with Prince Hall, and Caucasian males are associated with the Grand Lodge).

154. *Community Environment-Why is it that* the majority of the interviewees expressed that the majority of African-Americans of all ages are inevitably inclined to participate in a group performance dance routine at any function when certain musical tunes are played, (i.e., "The Electric Slide, The Chacha, and Wobble" themes)? Persons of the Caucasian Persuasion are not inclined to participate in group performance dance routines that are common in their social circles. However, when persons of Caucasian Persuasion participate (primarily southern) in line dancing, they dance to popular tune such as "Watermelon Crawl, Louisiana Saturday Night, or Achy Breaky Heart."

155. *Community Environment-Why is it that* the majority of the interviewees expressed that most male persons of the African-American Persuasion are not as enthused about the academic excellence of an African-American student who has achieved and has been offered multiple academic scholarships but will publicly rejoice with an overwhelming sense of enthusiasm if said student is awarded an athletic scholarship? Why is immeasurable emphasis placed on athletics when it is a given that most African-American students have the innate intellect to perform exceptionally well in academic subjects if given the attention at an early age? Conversely, most persons of the Caucasian Persuasion place less emphasis on athletics and more on academics.

156. *Community Environment-Why is it that* a growing number of young female persons of the African-American Persuasion allow themselves to be addressed as, or address each other as "bitches," " hoes," "tricks," or any other term defined as offensive and derogatory? Where is the self-respect?

157. *Community Environment-Why is it that* the majority of the interviewees expressed that most male persons of the African-American Persuasion are not as inclined to purchase chewing tobacco products as male persons of the Caucasian Persuasion?

158. *Community Environment-Why is it that* most male persons of the African-American Persuasion who purchase motorcycles for non-necessity purposes (leisure motorcycle enthusiast) are more prone to purchase mainly for its speed, potential acrobatic performance, color, and design and less for nostalgia purposes or the enjoyment of the carefree travel experience?

159. *Community Environment-Why is it that* the majority of the interviewees expressed that most Caucasians are more inclined to don attire (baseball cap and a long-sleeved shirt with sweater accompanied by short pants and sandals) that may be deemed nonsensical in weather that calls for full-body layered clothing? Conversely, most persons of the African-American Persuasion will don necessary clothing for said weather conditions.

160. ***Community Environment-Why is it that*** the majority of the interviewees expressed that most inner-city male and female persons of the African-American Persuasion allow aggravated assaults, homicides, street corner drug sales, burglaries, and strong armed assaults to continue in their communities when the victims or witnesses can unequivocally identify the assailant(s) and bring them to justice? Why is said community held hostage by its ethnic group by fearfully partaking in the code of silence and not wanting to be labeled as a "snitch?"

161. ***Community Environment-Why is it that*** the majority of the interviewees expressed that persons of the African-American Persuasion allow the British slave owner Willie Lynch's 1712 theory to continue to flourish in their communities by defining their destiny, controlling their economic prowess, limiting their political aspirations, impede educational advancements, and perpetuating other ill and non-constructive actions? It has been observed that most African-Americans allow any circumstance to discourage them or use circumstances as justification to not support each other. Sporting events such as K-12 or college basketball and football are the primary functions in which most African-Americans exhibit strong support for each other. Most persons of the Caucasian Persuasion support each other even with reluctance. However, if there is a choice between an African-American vendor and a Caucasian vendor with identical merchandise, the same education, and similar sales appeal, both ethnic groups believe the Caucasian vendor will generate more sales than the African-American vendor. Why?

162. ***Community Environment-Why is it that*** the majority of the interviewees expressed that persons of the African-American Persuasion are not taken seriously as political advisors or prime time commentators decidedly by persons of both the African-American and Caucasian Persuasions? This observation was triggered by the absences of African-American radio personalities, prime time political strategists, and television anchors. During the height of the nation's first African-American Democratic nominee's election, frequent appearances of African-American political commentators were common, and a few were granted opportunities to host their own shows. However, less than four months after electing the nation's first African-American President, those with shows for whatever reason (ratings perhaps) were canceled and again only a few appear to offer political debate on world views.

163. ***Community Environment-Why is it that*** persons of the African-American Persuasion are more encouraged to share their talents via prime time comedic venues and discouraged to partake in political, health, financial, or business prime-time venues? Why are network and cable media conglomerates inclined to limit or thwart the consistent display of intellect of African-Americans particularly on substantive political issues?

164. ***Community Environment-Why is it that*** the majority of the interviewees expressed that persons of the Caucasian Persuasion are featured with offers to exhibit multiple emotions and settings in art paintings whereas, most African-Americans are mostly in scenes that depict slavery, juke joints, poverty, and homelessness? Rarely are they portrayed in what one would consider positive images.

165. ***Community Environment-Why is it that*** the majority of the interviewees expressed that most male and female rap and pop artists of the African-American Persuasion consistently

center their lyrics around strong sexual overtones or emphasize subjects, such as oral sex, sexual positions (doggy style/hitting it from the back); licking her open thighs, laying her on her back, going downtown, put you to bed, legs in the air, turn her over, laying her down, tearing it up-all-night, beat it, and references to penis size (hangs long and low, thick trunk, can you get it up, big boy, pants getting bigger, is your pipe big enough, ride my joystick, built like a horse, etc.)? Why do the African-American communities allow their 8-17year old girls to consistently (day in and day out) hear such strong suggestive sexual language on predominantly African-American airwaves and expect them to grow up to respect themselves and fervidly reject louts in their communities that consistently recite the same language?

166. ***Community Environment-Why is it that*** the majority of the interviewees expressed that most persons of the Caucasian Persuasion are reserved in showing or expressing empathy regarding the African-American daily life experience? Why is it that most persons of the African-American Persuasion believe that most persons of the Caucasian Persuasion resent the notion that their past legal and law enforcement that accommodated their disdain for persons of the African-American Persuasion should not hinder their political, educational, and financial advancement? A hint of guilt is absurd and vehemently rejected.

167. ***Community Environment-Why is it that*** the majority of the interviewees expressed that the median income and net worth of most persons of the Caucasian Persuasion are approximately eighteen times that of persons of the African-American Persuasion? The Caucasian males' net worth exceeds the African-American males' net worth by double digits and is growing annually. Most of the interviewees believe that African-American males are significantly under employed or unemployed and lack a sound education. They also believe a

sizeable percent of African-American males are incarcerated, those who have been incarcerated are ineligible to vote to change policy, an overwhelming amount does not own businesses to grow wealth, and those who are interested in establishing businesses are systematically denied financing. Thus, the cycle continues from generation to generation.

168. ***Community Environment-Why is it that*** nearly every one of the interviewees expressed that persons of the African-American Persuasion are more inclined to back in parking lot spaces at retail centers more so than persons of the Caucasian Persuasion?

169. ***Community Environment-Why is it that*** most interviewees believe that most persons who are offspring of both the African-American and Caucasian Persuasion are the most likable, attractive, recruited, and marketable? Additionally, why are they more likely to be employed and considered for any medium of business advertisements by both persons of the African-American and Caucasian Persuasion who are interested in establishing diversity in their organization than persons who are solely of the African-American Persuasion?

170. ***Community Environment-Why is it that*** most of the interviewees expressed that the sheer presence of persons from offspring of African-Americans and Caucasian Americans partnerships or unions are social magnets that attract friends and associates (most people are attracted to them), they are offered more opportunities in general, experience a greater degree of persons seeking their friendship, accepted more frequently in various social organizations, given a greater edge in all levels of education, entertainment, sports, politics, and corporate America? They also receive leniency in the judicial system and are received with less resistance in efforts to defuse possible prejudicial occurrences between both ethnic groups. Why are they deemed ethnic mitigators?

171. Community Environment-Why is it that most of the interviewees expressed that persons of the African-American Persuasion, especially males, believe that they are targets for abuse and elimination by Caucasian male officers, regardless of the absence of weapons or firearms? They believe that no actions in an attempt to adhere to the demands of a Caucasian male officer will eventually result in acceptable use of deadly force by the officers. They also believe it is open season on any African-American male and deadly force is the officer's mitigation approach which enhances their case for acquittal if and only if they are charged or indicted.

172. Community Environment-Why is it that most of the interviewees expressed that persons of the Caucasian Persuasion have become insensitive to the slaying of African-American males by Caucasian male officers or other African-American males? They believe that African-American attack and slay each other over the minutest issues, and the African-American community does not become outraged or present any measures to forestall the violence among each other, so why should they care.

173. Community Environment-Why is it that most of the interviewees expressed that persons of the African-American Persuasion believe that the moment African-American officers apply deadly force towards an unarmed Caucasian male, extreme outrage will begin without delay? They believe that the African-American officers will be charged immediately, and indictment will be hastened. If African-American officers applied the use of deadly force on unarmed Caucasian males as frequently as past scenarios of Caucasian officers using deadly force on African-American males, governing bodies will hasten to restructure public policy to ensure the public that officers will be held accountable for their actions, and recruitment of African-American officers into police academies will be curtailed. Caucasians will definitively deem the African-American officer's action as retaliation from a plethora of excessive and deadly force scenarios of Caucasian male officers towards African-American males.

174. Community Environment-Why is it that most of the interviewees expressed that persons of the Caucasian Persuasion would not sacrifice "one" Caucasian male officer (right or wrong) in Ferguson, Missouri, Staten Island, New York, Cleveland, Ohio, Samford, Florida, New York, New York, Chicago, Illinois, Oakland, California, etc. to avoid total social chaos, destruction, distrust between communities and officers, the shredding of racial progress, vivid unveiling of racial prejudice, and the expenditure of millions of dollars used to repair or rebuild destroyed homes and businesses? Some interviewees of the Caucasian Persuasion expressed that an immediate arrest of just one officer would have perhaps prevented or defused boiling point racial tension and acrimony between both African-American and Caucasian communities.

175. Community Environment-Why is it that most of the interviewees expressed that persons of the African-American Persuasion reaction to injustices done to groups or individuals within their communities by persons of the Caucasian Persuasion are predictably followed by peaceful demonstration that eventually elevates to vandalism, destruction, looting, and heighten unrest? Interestingly, the destruction, vandalism, and looting are usually performed and contained in the very communities in which they live. Why do African-Americans destroy million dollars worth of property in their own communities as a protest of injustice caused by a handful of persons of the Caucasian Persuasion who reside in distant communities?

176. *Community Environment-Why is it that* most of the interviewees expressed that most male and female persons of the African-American Persuasion believe the "Black Lives Matter Movement" was indisputably introduced to bring national attention to the repeated killings of unarmed black males by Caucasians male and female officers, and it must cease? Historically, African-American communities have experienced frequent unnecessary and avoidable killings of unarmed African-American males for decades, but the actual killings were rarely made public (videos) until the public saw them broadcast firsthand multiple times. Why do African-Americans find it difficult to understand why most persons of the Caucasian persuasion seem to marginalize or feel offended by the "Black Lives Matter Movement" term or phase?

177. *Community Environment-Why is it that* most male and female Caucasian interviewees expressed that most African-American males (21 years and up) are considered docile when a Caucasian individual or firm repossesses their car, implements a home foreclosure, evicts his family from their home or apartment, belittles them publicly, purges them from higher education student enrollment, fires them from their job, or swindles them from payroll payments or any major financial depletion? They become bitter and angry, but they move on. However, they will take the life of another African-American male at the drop of a hat if they lose an argument, embarrassed publicly or if a friend or relative swindled them out of $20.00 or less.

178. *Community-Why is it that* most male and female African-American interviewees expressed that most Caucasian males and females develop a mindset that compels them to take whatever they choose from whomever they choose via legislation, litigation, corporate policy, lying, cheating or any other means as long as they author and dictate policies or regulations that will always benefit them? Most persons of the Caucasian Persuasion are desirous and quietly prefer residing in a core community that is solely of the Caucasian Persuasion while all other ethnic groups are to be peripheral and distant cohabitants. They incorporate obstacles to achieving the above desires, i.e., access to financing, income, private education academies, apartments and condominiums, gated communities, professional licensing, experience, etc. "Most African-Americans get it, but take pleasure in irritating and derailing their objective."

Chapter 5
Fashion

Fashion

This chapter is somewhat self-explanatory. There are distinct differences in fashion between African-Americans and Caucasian Americans that are routinely questioned by each ethnic group and sometimes within their ethnic camp. In interviewing numerous males and females of both ethnic persuasions, their observations and comments have been constructive for the most part. Conversely, some comments were not as constructive, but they possessed loads of humor. Fashion can be defined as the prevailing approach to style and trends frequent by multitudes of accepting opportunist. This chapter depicts inimitable styles and trends of both ethnic groups. An assortment of hair texture, color schemes and combinations, outer clothes wear combinations, and clothes and related complementary brand items are subjects that have been observed and garnered a significant amount of interest to make inquiries as to why the other ethnic groups wear what they wear. I was pleased to hear so many candid questions that brought attention to some of the smallest fashion details of both ethnic groups.

Admittedly, my observation of both ethnic groups from all social spheres of life and in numerous cities throughout the country revealed, that a vast majority of their unique styles and fashion between the two ethnic groups mirrored themselves in all parts of the country, and were not isolated to one region. Some will argue that all modes or styles are strictly regional, but I beg to differ. I refrain from the use of the word "all" simply for the fact that all is deemed conclusive and in very few instances can one emphatically use all as a final determination. During my interviews, all interviewees were not on the same accord, but most were, thus allowing me to define my interviews regarding fashion and other subjects as a result of most persons of the African-American and Caucasians Persuasions. My interviews were rather informative and enjoyable.

Interviewing students on several college campuses was an eye opener. African-Americans and Caucasian-Americans revealed some interesting fashion distinctions between the two ethnic groups. One particular distinction was that most females of the Caucasian Persuasion who donned athletic wear in 50 to 60-degree weather, usually wore a pair of sneakers with footies, white trimmed very loosely fitted athletic shorts, a simple tee shirt, and a lightweight jacket.

Most females of the African-American Persuasion who donned athletic wear in the same degree of weather wore sneakers with footies, a fitted warm-up suit or a pair of fitted shorts and jacket. Another distinction was most males of the Caucasian Persuasion donned a pullover polo shirt or short sleeve shirt with khaki shorts (above the knee) with loafers or open toe sandals. Most male African-Americans wore extra baggy shorts with lengths 8 to 10 inches below the knee or baggy jeans (some sagging) with immaculate sneakers, or open toe athletic sandals/slides with socks, and a polo pullover or hoodie.

African-American and Caucasian American female interviewees proceeded to share other clothing fashion distinctions worn in most any setting. They began to expound that most Caucasian Americans are more inclined to wear loose fitting clothes, whereas most African-American females are more inclined to don tightly fitted clothing in various settings. African-American females have a tendency to dress up to attend high school or college football games, whereas most Caucasian American females dress down to participate in the same kind of sporting event.

The above are just a few of my observations and welcoming responses I received from multiple individual and group interviews candidly conducted over the past several years. I am pleased to share with you more attention-grabbing observations and that perhaps these observations will spark constructive dialogue. These represent the majority of interviewees and my observations.

Fashion Observations / Differences

Picture This

1. *Fashion-Why is it that* most of the interviewees expressed that most male and female persons of the Caucasian Persuasion who wear baggy or over- sized pants rarely maintain their clothing in good condition? These articles of clothing are usually and purposely grimy, exhibit detached hems, and are considered unpleasant. Conversely, persons of the African-American Persuasion don the same type of clothing but maintain their clothing in good condition. Their clothes are usually clean, ironed, starched or even dry-cleaned, regardless of their socioeconomic status or financial circumstances.

2. *Fashion-Why is it that* most of the interviewees expressed that persons of the Caucasian Persuasion in the fashion industry relentlessly and unyieldingly promote psychological illusions that define the perfect female specimen? In each instance, a perfect specimen is a person of the Caucasian Persuasion with a boyish figure that is a minimum of 5 feet 8 inches tall with small breasts, hips, one hundred ten pounds soaking wet, long torso, and legs.

3. *Fashion-Why is it that* most of the interviewees expressed that persons of the Caucasian Persuasion persistently advertise sports cars, mechanical tools, and sports magazines that display Caucasian females whose body attributes are considerably opposite of what the fashion industry depicts? In both the fashion industry and male sports advertising medium, female persons of the African-American Persuasion are rarely spotlighted.

4. ***Fashion-Why is it that*** most of the interviewees expressed
    that some female persons of the African-American Persuasion
    purchase hair extensions that do not remotely match their
    existing hair texture, elasticity or color, but will wear it proudly
    even if they look somewhat bizarre?

5. ***Fashion-Why is it that*** most of the interviewees expressed
    that some female persons of the African-American Persuasion
    who weigh at least 250 lbs. to 300 lbs. have "no shame in their
    game," particularly when they wear the brightest, tightest, and
    sheerest spandex pants, jeans, halter tops or blouses with their
    entire cellulite-filled arms and legs exposed?

6. ***Fashion-Why is it that*** most of the interviewees expressed that
    some female persons of the Caucasian Persuasion who weigh
    at least 250 lbs. to 300 lbs. have "no shame in their game,"
    especially when they parade around in their swimwear that
    shows every unsightly crack, roll, crevice, and layer of fat that
    their body has ever produced?

7. ***Fashion-Why is it that*** most of the interviewees expressed
    that some female persons of the African-American Persuasion
    apparently try to look as bad as they can when running an
    errand to the local grocery store, pharmacy, or mall by wearing
    neon multicolored hair rollers, a food-stained blouse, pants
    or a skirt that is at least three sizes too small, legs that are
    embarrassingly lotion-free, and open heel fluffy house shoes
    exposing their yet again lotion-free and unpleasant cracked
    heels?

8. ***Fashion-Why is it that*** most of the interviewees expressed
    that most male persons of the Caucasian Persuasion don khaki
    pants (dress, casual wear or shorts) more frequently than male
    persons of the African-American Persuasion?

9.   ***Fashion-Why is it that*** most of the interviewees expressed that most female persons of the African-American Persuasion who don Yves Saint-Laurent, Georgio Gucci, Coco Chanel, Louis Vuitton, and other expensive ($500.00 - $1,700.00) purses and are lower range hourly wage employees, truly believe their close acquaintances and John Q. Public are in awe of their exceptional purchases? Conversely, most female persons of the Caucasian Persuasion that have hourly wage jobs seem not to be remotely interested in any purchase of that kind just to attempt to convince their acquaintances that their hourly wages comfortably affords them the luxury of having the finest of accessories.

10.   ***Fashion-Why is it that*** most of the interviewees expressed that most male persons of the Caucasian Persuasion who are career governmental workers, rarely wear tee shirts under their dress shirts even in business or formal attire more so than male persons of the African-American Persuasion?

11.   ***Fashion-Why is it that*** most of the interviewees expressed that most male persons of the Caucasian Persuasion wear short sleeve dress shirts more frequently in a business setting than male persons of the African-American Persuasion?

12.   ***Fashion-Why is it that*** most of the interviewees expressed that most persons of the African-American Persuasion have a very small percentage, if any or ownership in hair, nail, and clothing supply companies, but as consumers, they are among the highest in purchasing power? Why is it that they will frequent said businesses and spend plenty of money, but are unable or not desirous to own similar businesses?

13.   ***Fashion-Why is it that*** most of the interviewees expressed that most parents of Caucasian females between the ages of 2 to 10 years old don their daughter's hair with one massive sized hair bow at social functions that encourage and require dress

attire? Seldom do they allow or use more than one hair bow/ hair accessory.

14. ***Fashion-Why is it that*** most of the interviewees expressed that most parents of African-American females between the ages of 2 to 10 years old don their daughter's hair with multicolored, multiple hair bows and barrettes that appear to be painfully affixed? Seldom do they allow or use one hair bow/hair accessory.

15. ***Fashion-Why is it that*** most of the interviewees expressed that most male persons of the African-American Persuasion who wear oversized baggy and saggy pants work unnecessarily to travel about by holding their pants up with their hand(s) and walk wide legged? They refuse to, or consider it unfashionable to wear the appropriate clothing accessories (i.e., a belt) that support pants? However, when they do wear proper belts, the deep and low sagging persists. Why do they repeatedly wish to support their well-ironed or dry-cleaned pants with their hand(s) as they walk? Their actions have frequently invited cruel verbal expressions from both persons of the Caucasian and African-American Persuasions who have expressed that they are perplexed by this "flaunting of ignorance."

16. ***Fashion-Why is it that*** most of the interviewees revealed that most male persons of the African-American Persuasion who happen to border the poverty level, or lower middle class wear massive ear studs that are no less than one karat or two karats in size? Why do they expect their peers and others to believe that they have acquired a significant amount of money for the real clarity, color, and cut of a genuine diamond? Why is this deemed such an interest?

17. ***Fashion-Why is it that*** most of the interviewees expressed that an alarming number of young persons of the Caucasian Persuasion carry out their desires to artificially alter their

physical appearances to look like their favorite actor, singer or popular television personality? Why are the parents allowing their kids to undergo these expensive, invasive, and unnecessary surgeries just for sheer vanity? Conversely, most persons of the African-American Persuasion of a similar age bracket may have desires and the financial resources to follow through, but they choose to maintain their birth appearances and features.

18. ***Fashion-Why is it that*** most of the interviewees expressed that most male persons of the African-American Persuasion rarely wear open toe sandals during the spring or summer seasons? Notwithstanding, those that desire to wear casual sandals or sports slippers hardly expose their feet; they are usually accompanied by socks. Additionally, most African-American males believe that the purity of their masculinity is removed or compromised if they don open toe sandals.

19. ***Fashion-Why is it that*** most of the interviewees expressed that a male person of the Caucasian Persuasion five o'clock shadow is regarded as provocative and sexually attractive? However, a male person of the African-American Persuasion five o'clock shadow is rarely seen, but if seen, it is regarded as characteristic of one who is lazy or one with poor hygiene.

20. ***Fashion-Why is it that*** most of the interviewees expressed that most persons of the Caucasian Persuasion who are entrenched in the hip-hop or rap music industry do not don gold or platinum teeth "grills" that are commonly displayed among male persons of the African American Persuasion within said music industry?

21. ***Fashion-Why is it that*** most of the interviewees expressed that most women of the Caucasian Persuasion rarely or never style their hair in a design that is commonly called a "freeze,"

comparable to that of female persons of the African American Persuasion?

22. ***Fashion-Why is it that*** most of the interviewees expressed that most women of the African American Persuasion rarely or never style their hair in a design that is commonly called a "tease," comparable to that of female persons of the Caucasian Persuasion?

23. ***Fashion-Why is it that*** most of the interviewees expressed that most men of the Caucasian Persuasion rarely or never wear purple, apple red, canary yellow, royal blue, lime green or all white dress suits with matching shoes to worship services or functions that require dress attire? However, an African-American male will be more inclined to do so.

24. ***Fashion-Why is it that*** most of the interviewees expressed that most female persons of the African American Persuasion frequently express that they are going to schedule an appointment at the "beauty shop" to get their hair "did?" Most female persons of the Caucasian Persuasion frequently express that they are going to schedule an appointment at the "beauty salon" to get their hair "done."

25. ***Fashion-Why is it that*** most of the interviewees expressed that most African American males who are over forty years of age refuse to accept their actual age by wearing hip-hop clothing, (i.e., extremely baggy pants, oversized white tees, stocking caps, du-rags, and head bandanas with baseball caps slanted 15° to 45° from front and center of their head)? Older (fortyish) females of both the African-American and Caucasian Persuasions ask; is this attire entirely inappropriate for a 40-year-old male regardless of his ethnicity?

26. ***Fashion-Why is it that*** most of the interviewees expressed that most women of the Caucasian Persuasion are more inclined to don larger purses which are usually above standard size more so than most women of the African-American Persuasion?

27. ***Fashion-Why is it that*** most of the interviewees expressed that most persons of the African-American Persuasion, when attending a college football or basketball sporting event, have a tendency to dress up? On the contrary, persons of the Caucasian Persuasion have a tendency to dress casual or dress down?

28. ***Fashion-Why is it that*** most of the interviewees expressed that most females of the African-American Persuasion are more inclined to grow fingernails that are at least 2 inches long or longer or purchase fingernail extensions that are also 2 inches or longer more so than females of the Caucasian Persuasion?

29. ***Fashion-Why is it that most*** of the interviewees expressed that most females of the African-American Persuasion are more inclined than females of the Caucasian Persuasion to spend an exorbitant amount of money to purchase designer fingernails?

30. ***Fashion-Why is it that*** most of the interviewees expressed that most females of the African-American Persuasion purchase expensive designer clothing that are designed by mostly persons of the Caucasian Persuasion? In most cases, they cannot name at least five African-American fashion designers, but can proudly and effortlessly name at least ten to fifteen Caucasian designers.

31. ***Fashion-Why is it that*** most of the interviewees expressed that persons of the African-American Persuasion seem to be more inclined to wear house shoes and hair rollers in public (i. e., grocery stores, malls, service stations, post offices, and most frequently, convenient stores)? On the contrary, persons

of the Caucasian Persuasion seem to be less inclined to slip on house shoes or don hair rollers in public settings. However, most African-Americans do not go about business or shopping shirtless (males) or barefoot in public as mostly done by Caucasians.

32. ***Fashion-Why is it that*** most of the interviewees expressed that male persons of the African-American Persuasion who are a part of the hip-hop culture don, more frequently than any other colors, red, black, blue, and white?

33. ***Fashion-Why is it that*** most of the interviewees expressed that male persons of the African-American Persuasion who are a part of the hip-hop culture don the same clothing summer and winter? In most cases, their attire is not distinguishable from winter season or summer season, only with the exception of a sweater or coat.

34. ***Fashion-Why is it that*** nearly every one of the interviewees expressed that most male persons of the African-American Persuasion who are influenced by the hip-hop or rap culture rarely wear short pants above the knee or just below the knee? In most cases, they wear excessively baggy short pants that extend to the shin or below the shin. Conversely, most male persons of the Caucasian Persuasion of all ages (with the exception of most athletes) wear moderately loose shorts pants usually above the knee or just below the knee.

35. ***Fashion-Why is it that*** nearly every one of the interviewees expressed that most persons of the African-American Persuasion believe the fashion industry works feverishly to search, secure, and label female models who happen to have blue or green eyes and blonde hair as America's top models? Why does the above description consistently and noticeably reference persons of the Caucasian Persuasion?

I Couldn't Believe It Either

36. *Fashion-Why is it that* nearly every one of the interviewees expressed that most persons of the Caucasian Persuasion believe that the fashion industry fears loss of sales, popularity, and funding if the supermodel ranking of African-American males and females exceeds fifteen percent?

37. *Fashion-Why is it that* nearly every one of the interviewees expressed that most persons of the Caucasian Persuasion describe mainly Caucasian female supermodels as gorgeous and beautiful? Clearly, most persons of the Caucasian Persuasion depict most African-American female supermodels as exotic, strong, ones with beautiful chocolate skin, and runway queens, but seldom describe them as gorgeous or strikingly beautiful.

38. *Fashion-Why is it that* nearly every one of the interviewees expressed that most persons of the African-American Persuasion define an African-American male who happens to wear a snug fitting undershirt, short pants above the knee, and open toe sandals as feminine? Both persons of the African-American and Caucasian Persuasions rarely tag Caucasian males who wear the exact attire as described above as feminine.

39. *Fashion-Why is it that* nearly every one of the interviewees expressed that most female persons of the African-American Persuasion 250 lbs. to 300 lbs. are becoming more confident or comfortable, donning exceedingly snug sleeveless blouses exposing their sizeable arms? Frequent observations reveal most persons of the Caucasian Persuasion 250 lbs. to 300 lbs. are more inclined to wear tight upper body clothing that exposes their midsection.

40. *Fashion-Why is it that* nearly every one of the interviewees expressed that male persons of the Caucasian Persuasion who are balding but maintain long hair insist on donning a comb-over instead of accepting natural hair loss?

41. ***Fashion-Why is it that*** nearly every one of the interviewees expressed that most young males of the African-American Persuasion purchase shorts, dress or a casual pair of pants that are at least three sizes larger than their waist to only emulate an inmate's style of sagging similarly to state or federal issued uniforms? Most young males sagging have exceeded the waist size and have introduced a vertical differential that has given reason to expose their athletic shorts and underwear. Why is it that older African-American males believe that younger males whose pants rest far below the waist exposing their underwear and often buttocks are extending invitations with multiple connotations? Most believe state and federally issued uniforms may not fit as comfortably as one perhaps is accustom. But an individual that is "free" purposely sag exceedingly below their waist fully exposing their buttock and underwear and holding their pants up with their hand or with a belt, it may be challenging for them to demand "respect" from anyone and project the "I'm hard" or I'm a gangsta" disposition. Why is it that most African-American females are not impressed with said attire but are overwhelmingly interested in males of any persuasion that wear comfortably loose-fitting clothes that accentuate their chest, abdominal muscles, waist, and glutes or, plainly put, an athletic cut?

42. ***Fashion-Why is it that*** nearly every one of the interviewees expressed that most older males and females of both the African-American and Caucasian Persuasions believe that those who don extreme sagging pants and oversized clothes have a simple form of self-dislike and undeniably are ashamed of his/her body? If most females expressly signify their dislike for such attire, then who is the intended party, principally when the convexity of the buttocks and underwear are exposed?

43. ***Fashion-Why is it that*** nearly every one of the interviewees expressed that most male persons of the African-American Persuasion of modest means place significant importance on sneakers/basketball shoes? Most have at least four pairs of expensive sneakers/basketball shoes, all of which are immaculate. Additionally, their sensitivity to one being marred intentionally or unintentionally by another male person is heightened tenfold to a level that may cause physical harm or loss of life to the accuser. In most cases, their initial purchase of the sneaker/basketball shoes is strictly to meet a fashion need and not to be used for its intended purpose (official or recreational sports activities). After the newness of the shoes has worn off, then and only then will they be used for their intended purpose.

44. ***Fashion-Why is it that*** nearly every one of the interviewees expressed that most female persons of the African-American Persuasion avoid simplicity when after five or evening wear is requested at special functions? In most cases, the African-American female will don a sequined type dress with matching hat, purse, and shoes in lieu of a simple black, blue, or red A-line dress. Additionally, the interviewees expressed that many African-American females have a tendency to over accessorize.

45. ***Fashion-Why is it that*** nearly every one of the interviewees expressed that most persons of the Caucasian Persuasion question why the older males of the African-American Persuasion have allowed young African-American males in the lower socioeconomic demographics to wear excessive sagging and oversized pants while purposely exposing their underwear at most any function in or out of their communities?

46. ***Fashion-Why is it that*** nearly every one of the interviewees expressed that most persons of the Caucasian Persuasion have

allowed the camouflage hunter green attire, rebel flag posting, and cross bar combinations to vividly represent the poorly educated and their deep hatred of other ethnic groups to run widespread in their communities?

47. ***Fashion-Why is it that*** nearly every one of the interviewees expressed that male and female persons of the Caucasian Persuasion have allowed the gothic attire to run rampant in their communities?

48. ***Fashion-Why is it that*** nearly every one of the interviewees expressed that most young female persons of the African-American Persuasion don earrings that appear to be quite heavy and extra-large? However, most young female persons of the Caucasian Persuasion rarely wear heavy and oversized accessories.

49. ***Fashion-Why is it that*** nearly every one of the interviewees expressed that most females of the Caucasian Persuasion do not wear stockings/pantyhoses at functions that require dress or black tie attire, whereas most females of the African-American Persuasion wear stockings/pantyhose and slips at the same semi-formal function?

50. **Fashion-Why is it that** nearly every one of the interviewees expressed that most young males of the African-American Persuasion wear their dress pants six to eight inches longer than what may be considered customary or appropriate length?

51. ***Fashion-Why is it that*** nearly every one of the interviewees expressed that most females of the African-American Persuasion who happen to be reality show personalities wear hair weaves, extensions, and other hair attachments that are unusually long? Interviewees have also expressed that their idea of dressing up sends an injurious message to younger female

African-Americans that long hair is required and essential to displaying beauty and being accepted.

52. ***Fashion-Why is it that*** nearly every one of the interviewees expressed that most African-American males between the age to 12 to 35 place extraordinary emphases and money in purchasing athletic footwear primarily basketball shoes (more than ten pairs) and occasionally deem themselves basketball shoe collectors.

53. ***Fashion-Why is it that*** nearly every one of the female African-American and Caucasian American interviewees are more attracted to African-American males over 21 that sport dreadlocks at shoulder length worn in a full or split ponytail style? Other non-dreadlock hair styles they admire are the businessman's twist with fade, crew cut, and the simple buzz cut styles.

54. ***Fashion-Why is it that*** nearly every one of the interviewees expressed that most male and female persons of the Caucasian Persuasion of legal age are more inclined than male and female persons of the African-American Persuasion to don multiple piercing, tattoo shelves, full head and body tattoos, racial symbols, chronology of life changes and experiences, eyeball tattoos, and ear gauges?

55. ***Fashion-Why is it that*** nearly every one of the interviewees expressed that they are profoundly perplexed by the rigidity of most African-American males that proudly don severe sagging exposing at least three-quarters of their buttocks but deem the idea of wearing open toe sandals notably compromise their concept of masculinity? Conversely and particularly, most African-American and Caucasian female interviewees believe most African-American males that wear open toe sandals project confidently and soundly a more masculine appeal

than most African-American males that brazenly don severe sagging exposing their buttocks. The interviewees continue to ask the question, "is showing their ass all day with your boyz a good thang?" or "if the brothas can recognize their ass (style of underwear, buttock curvature, and projection) a block away, has the premise masculinity been compromised?"

56. *Fashion-Why is it that* nearly every one of the interviewees expressed that most male persons of the African-American Persuasion between the ages of 12 - 35 are more inclined to don un-tucked tee-shirts and dress shirts, sagging pants, untied and unlaced shoe strings, exposed shoe tongues, flat bib snapbacks/ caps with tag labels attached, jacket hoodies front edge resting on the crown of their heads more so than male persons of the Caucasian Persuasion?

57. *Fashion-Why is it that* nearly every one of the interviewees expressed that mainly the poorly educated and non-professional African-American females spend most of their money (conspicuous consumption which equates to elevated status in their communities) on hair extensions, extras long wigs, eyelashes, fingernails, toenails, shoes, luxury handbags, inexpensive jewelry and accessories, and designer clothes? In doing so, most Caucasian interviewees questioned why their preoccupation with an inclination toward the purchasing of consumer goods was usually expended among multiple ethnic communities except the African-American communities?

58. *Fashion-Why is it that* nearly every one of the interviewees expressed that mainly the poorly educated and non-professional Caucasian females spend little to no money (do not engage in conspicuous consumption) on hair extensions, extras long wigs, eyelashes, fingernails, toenails, shoes, luxury handbags, inexpensive jewelry and accessories, and designer clothes?

Chapter 6
Sports

Sports

This chapter accentuates observations and interpretations of hundreds of African-Americans and Caucasian Americans, males and females equally, that I have interviewed across the country. My observations and interpretations are in sync with the interviewees as well. Sports have such a varied field of activity. There are so many amazing sports and athletes that have profound effects on our lives in stories that are incredibly encouraging, and some rather disappointing. Most of the interviewees have personally identified with the bulk of inquiry interests that I have amassed in this chapter. The interviewees and I believe the sports industry is governed and controlled by mostly persons of the Caucasian persuasion, and the bulk of the athletes are a little more diverse. It is given that particular sports have a stronger participation of African-Americans while other sports have a more robust participation of Caucasian Americans.

The collegiate and professional sports industries are major stakeholders in some local and state economies. Admittedly, the more popular sports such as baseball, track and field, basketball, and football usually have a greater impact. Winning teams often solidify hope and potential growth for some local economies. When the sports team wins, the locals win. The individual team athlete's personalities, good or bad, draw spectators to sporting events, enhance the team's support, and fuel the local economy. As for most industries, the "dollar" influences control and power, and the persons or entities that issue the checks are usually the ones who are in control.

As for the collegiate division, the interviewees have all expressed that they believe mainstream America is intricately and emotionally involved in collegiate sports. One collegiate sport in particular that significantly invokes passionate loyalty is NCAA football. The interviewees recognized the multi-million dollars football division of the NCAA and the influence it has on universities, coaches, and student-athletes. The majority of interviewees broached the issue of public universities top administrators relinquishing their authority and control to appease openhandedly the head football coach and influential alumni. This transfer of power allows the head football coach to dictate actions he or she will and will not do. The interviewees have vehemently expressed their concerns about the larger-than-life salaries of a handful of collegiate athletic conference coaches when the collegiate athlete compensation is not seriously considered.

The interviewees have captured two sides of the debate of coaches and their staff appropriate compensation which are predominately of the Caucasian persuasion versus student-athletes' appropriate compensation and graduation rates, especially athletes of the African-American Persuasion. Surprisingly, the debate amongst the interviewees reversed some mindsets of their previous perceptions and limited knowledge about the issue mentioned above. This particular chapter speaks to not only the issue as noted earlier but multiple sports explorations that both African-Americans and Caucasian Americans have questioned and vied for constructive dialogue and debate. Some inquiries may seem humorous while others may take on a more serious connotation. It is my hope that all inquiries will allay cognitive dissonance and infuse an unhindered understanding of each ethnic group's idiosyncrasies. These questions represent the interviewees and my observations.

Sports Observations / Differences

Let The Truth Be Known

1. ***Sports-Why is it that*** most of the interviewees expressed that persons of the African-American Persuasion rarely serve as athletic directors at universities and colleges where the majority student enrollment is of the Caucasian Persuasion? Also, why is it that persons of the Caucasian Persuasion rarely serve as athletic directors at universities and colleges where the majority student enrollment is of the African-American Persuasion?

2. ***Sports-Why is it that*** most of the interviewees expressed that male persons of the African-American Persuasion who make up approximately 50% of the active participation in professional sports, i.e., NBA 76%, MBA 8%, and NFL 66%, and have excelled financially but have yet to acquire more than 51% (excluding Mr. Michael Jordan's approximate 89% ownership of the Charlotte Hornets) ownership or serve in a significant leadership position in the front offices of the three professional sports league organizations? Their combined ownership is approximately less than 10%.

3. ***Sports-Why is it that*** most of the interviewees expressed that male athletes of the African-American Persuasion, who are students at Predominantly White Institutions, are only respected in the season in which their sport is engaged as participants, but are treated entirely different when they are not running up or down a basketball court or football field? But during such time, all other non-sports playing male African-Americans are demeaned and belittled, but as an acceptable justification, the common expression is "you are different from them; the others that is."

4.   ***Sports-Why is it that*** most of the interviewees expressed that most male persons of the African-American Persuasion who are talented and have the physical attributes to complete a basketball dunk successfully, intimidate their competition by hanging two to three seconds from the goal rim and shake their groin area in their opponents' faces? However, male persons of the Caucasian Persuasion rarely display this method of intimidation.

5.   ***Sports-Why is it that*** most of the interviewees expressed that male persons of the Caucasian Persuasion recently deem African-American college and professional football head coaches and quarterbacks as legitimate, astute, accomplished, and applauded leaders, but just 25 years ago, they expressed negative and opposing thoughts, such as, "they did not have the intellect to perform in these high salaried and most important positions?"

6.   ***Sports-Why is it that*** most of the interviewees expressed that most male persons of the Caucasian Persuasion, who are collegiate sports enthusiasts, perform extreme acts to express their male bonding and support of their school's team, (i.e., painting their naked chests and displaying them in either sub-temperature of sweltering heat, streaking, participating in beer binging, and mascot kidnapping and defacing)?

7.   ***Sports-Why is it that*** most of the interviewees expressed that most professional basketball franchises have, and are dominated by male players of the African-American Persuasion, but in the past three years, more male persons of the Caucasian Persuasion from foreign countries are partaking in and are becoming favorable alternatives in the annual league draft sessions?

8. ***Sports-Why is it that*** most of the interviewees expressed that male sports enthusiasts of the African-American Persuasion are not inclined to paint their naked topless bodies with letters, numbers, or any other phrases at a high school, collegiate or professional sporting events? Additionally, the acts as mentioned above are usually performed in all kinds of extreme weather conditions.

9. ***Sports-Why is it that*** most of the interviewees expressed that multiple male persons of the African-American Persuasion have been noted mainly for their athletic mastery in baseball, basketball, track and field, and football, but not swimming, tennis, soccer, golf, hockey, snow skiing, water skiing, fishing, cycling, ice skating, snowboarding, curling, skateboarding, gymnastics, equestrianism, or motor car racing?

10. ***Sports-Why is it that*** most of the interviewees expressed that most NBA African-American males are becoming noticeably decorated with tattoos? Conversely, most NBA Caucasian males (with the exception of Chris "Birdman" Andersen) are not donning tattoos that are of such size that it creates a distraction for television viewers, and courtside spectators as do African-American males. What are the African-American male athletes conveying to impressionable young sports enthusiasts?

11. ***Sports-Why is it that*** most of the interviewees expressed that most male African-American professional soccer athletes are fiercely disliked by male persons of the Caucasian Persuasion in Europe and the Middle East to the point that their lives are threatened just because of their ethnicity?

12. ***Sports-Why is it that*** most of the interviewees expressed that most male Caucasian athletes are featured more often in *Sports Illustrated, Men's Health, Workout,* and most exercise and fitness magazines than African-American male athletes when

emphases are placed on sheer fitness? Are African-American male collegiate or professional athletes as marketable as Caucasian athletes?

13. ***Sports-Why is it that*** most of the interviewees expressed that most females of both African-American and Caucasian Persuasions are physically attracted to most collegiate and professional male African-American athletes that are six feet tall or taller more so than Caucasian athletes with the similar physical build and height?

14. ***Sports-Why is it that*** most of the interviewees expressed that an increasing amount of African-American professional male athletes are becoming aggressively (publicly) dissatisfied with their lucrative and multi-year contracts more so than Caucasian male athletes? Some African-American professional male athletes publicly express arrogantly that a mere one, two or three million-dollars loss in contract disputes is deemed insignificant.

15. ***Sports-Why is it that*** most of the interviewees expressed that most African-American male and female athletes are described as having innate athletic abilities more so than most Caucasian male and female athletes? Most sports commentators explain a significant amount of Caucasian athletic masteries as being of those who worked hard and trained many hours and years to develop their excellence. They rarely equate their athletic superiority with attributes that are innate in their make-up.

16. ***Sports-Why is it that*** most of the interviewees expressed that African-American males have been deemed the majority of professional athletes in the NBA-30 teams and NFL-32 teams for the past 20 years but only make-up less than 45% of head coaches (approximately 43%+ in the NBA - 10%+ in the NFL) in the industry? Are NFL owners still reluctant to hiring

first-time African-American head coaches in comparison to their consistent practice of hiring first-time Caucasian head coaches subsequent to the introduction of the Rooney Rule?

17. ***Sports-Why is it that*** most of the interviewees expressed that most African-American and Caucasian male and female professional athletes have been, or are advised by mostly sports agents of the Caucasian Persuasion and are seldom managed by persons of the African-American Persuasion? What is the percentage of male and female Caucasian and African-American professional athletes that are advised by African-American sports agents? Most interviewees believe African-American sports agents manage approximately 18% of all professional athletes and Caucasian sports agents manage approximately 82%. Why the wide disparity?

18. ***Sports-Why is it that*** most of the interviewees expressed that most professional Caucasian male athletes, who retire from their prospective sport, experience what one would define as a smooth or uneventful transition from athlete to entrepreneur? Conversely, most professional African-American male athletes experience substantial difficulty in making the transition from athlete to entrepreneur.

19. ***Sports-Why is it that*** most of the interviewees expressed that most new and seasoned African-American NFL quarterbacks are paid significantly less than Caucasian NFL quarterbacks with equal or less experience, especially with business endorsements?

20. ***Sports-Why is it that*** most of the interviewees expressed that most African-American high school, collegiate, and professional male athletes do not value the importance of education equally as most Caucasian male athletes? Most Caucasian male athletes develop a plan "B" to further their studies if their athletic

aspirations are not fulfilled; whereas most African-American male athletes depend heavily on their athleticism and relinquish the notion of establishing a plan "B" to advance their education if they fall short of realizing their athletic dreams.

21. ***Sports-Why is it that*** most of the interviewees expressed that a significant amount of observers accept as true that African-American females are often outnumbered and less successful in their aggression in establishing sexual relations or securing marital status with professional African-American male athletes than Caucasian females?

22. ***Sports-Why is it that*** most of the interviewees expressed that most African-American male adult athletes allowed their public unprofessional attire (pop culture/hip-hop/gangsta attire) during media events to deteriorate to the point that the NBA Commissioner had to introduce and reinforce a policy to prevent further public professional attire deterioration?

23. **Sports-Why is it that** most of the interviewees expressed that most Caucasian male athletes signing bonuses, contract negotiations, contract amount and terms are not publicized as frequently as those of most African-American male athletes? Many sports commentators conveniently announce more often African-Americans salaries with a hint of sarcasm than those of Caucasian male athletes. "This guy, with all that money.... Why did he do what he did?"

24. ***Sports-Why is it that*** most of the interviewees expressed that most African-American high school, collegiate, and professional male athletes are more inclined to place extra emphases on grooming, (i.e., applying lotion, cologne, oils, precision cut hairlines, mustaches, and beards than most Caucasian male athletes)?

25. ***Sports-Why is it that*** most of the interviewees expressed that most African-American collegiate and professional male athletes are more secure, unabashed and unaffected by full nudity exposure or putting on view their genitalia/endowment among other athletes in community showers than male athletes of the Caucasian Persuasion?

26. ***Sports-Why is it that*** the majority of the interviewees expressed that most African-American collegiate and professional male athletes exert greater effort to be acknowledged as phenomenal or exceptional by exhibiting glaring acrobatic flare when dunking a basketball than the Caucasian male athletes?

27. ***Sports-Why is it that*** the majority of the interviewees expressed that most Caucasian collegiate and professional male athletes are more prone to shave their bodies or remove all hair from their bodies than African-American male athletes?

28. **Sports-Why is it that** the majority of the interviewees expressed that most Caucasian collegiate male athletes are more inclined not to wear shower sandals in community showers than African-American male athletes?

29. ***Sports-Why is it that*** the majority of the interviewees expressed that most African-American high school, collegiate and professional male athletes are more self-encouraged to develop their physiques for endurance, strength, and mainly vanity (chest, biceps, triceps, abdominal muscles, quadriceps, etc.) than Caucasian male athletes? Why is it that most African-American male athletes believe the possession of a "cut physique" is as important as strength and training workouts?

30. ***Sports-Why is it that*** the majority of the interviewees expressed that most African-American male athletes are more

predisposed to chew gum during practice and an official game competition than Caucasian male athletes?

31. ***Sports-Why is it that*** the majority of the interviewees expressed that most professional African-American male athletes place emphasis and assessment on their dress attire (tailored, name brand, and unique stylishness of patterns and color selections) before and after sports competitions more so than Caucasian male athletes?

32. ***Sports-Why is it that*** the majority of the interviewees expressed that most African-American male collegiate and professional athletes have more motivation to train and to weight lift than most Caucasian male athletes?

33. ***Sports-Why is it that*** the majority of the interviewees expressed that most African-American collegiate male athletes have a closer relationship with an African-American male coach than Caucasian collegiate male athletes have with a Caucasian male coach?

34. ***Sports-Why is it that*** the majority of the interviewees believe most African-American collegiate and professional female and male athletes work notably harder to exceed performance execution expectations for a coach of the Caucasian Persuasion than for a coach of the African-American Persuasion?

35. ***Sports-Why is it that*** the majority of the interviewees expressed that most African-American and Caucasian high school, collegiate and professional female and male athletes believe that most African-American coaches are more sincere, trustworthy, and caring about their well-being than Caucasian coaches?

36. **Sports-Why is it that** the majority of the interviewees expressed that most African-American high school, collegiate

and professional male and female athletes anticipate and are encouraged by African-American coaches to hold them to a higher performance standard?

37. ***Sports-Why is it that*** the majority of the interviewees expressed that most African-American male athletes are more likely to intimidate their opponents by "trash talking" more so than most Caucasian male athletes?

38. ***Sports-Why is it that*** the majority of the interviewees believe that most Caucasian male basketball athletes demonstrate basketball fundamentals more consistently and are likely to be more accurate free throw, two point, and three point shooters than most African-American male basketball athletes?

39. ***Sports-Why is it that*** the majority of the interviewees expressed that most African-American male basketball athletes are likely to be more agile and better jumpers than Caucasian male basketball athletes?

40. ***Sports-Why is it that*** the majority of the interviewees expressed that most Caucasian male athletes or fitness enthusiasts are more prone to arrive at a gym in groups more so than most African-American male athletes or fitness enthusiasts?

41. ***Sports-Why is it that*** the majority of the interviewees expressed that most African-American male athletes are more apt to wear more athletic clothing, i.e., two layers of upper body under shirts and at least three pairs of lower body gym warm-ups or shorts, than Caucasian male athletes?

42. ***Sports-Why is it that*** the majority of the interviewees expressed that most Caucasian male athletes or fitness enthusiasts are more inclined to use community whirlpools, steam rooms, and saunas before or after workout sessions more so than African-American male athletes or fitness enthusiasts?

43. ***Sports-Why is it that*** the majority of the interviewees expressed that most African-American male athletes who are participants in team sports are more prone to exhibit or project an "it's all about me" complex or narcissistic disposition than most Caucasian male athletes? In most scenarios, a team's spirit and holistic approach to triumph is usually not the consequence of one or two African-American males' athletic performances. A team' triumph is usually a consequence of excellent team chemistry, collective adroitness, and individual selflessness.

44. ***Sports-Why is it that*** the majority of the interviewees expressed that most collegiate African-American male athletes who look up to Caucasian coaches as father figures, especially those with the absence of a father in their homes, will accept higher levels of verbal humiliation from them than they will from African-American coaches?

45. ***Sports-Why is it that*** the majority of the interviewees expressed that most collegiate African-American male athletes who open up to their Caucasian coach about personal and social matters during regular game season, i.e., basketball, baseball, football, etc., find it difficult to feel welcomed by the same coach at the completion of the regular season?

46. ***Sports-Why is it that*** the majority of the interviewees expressed that most high school and collegiate Caucasian male athletes are more inclined to perform nude pranks and are more physically playful with each other in locker rooms, dorm rooms, and community showers than African-American male athletes?

47. ***Sports-Why is it that*** the majority of the interviewees expressed that most high school African-American male athletes are more driven to work harder to perfect their athletic talent in hopes to secure an athletic scholarship more so than Caucasian male athletes? Additionally, why do most high school

African-American athletes believe the only road to college is through athletics more so than most high school Caucasian athletes?

48. *Sports-Why is it that* the majority of the interviewees expressed that most collegiate African-American male athletes rarely consider professional beach volleyball as a profession?

49. *Sports-Why is it that* the majority of the interviewees expressed that most college and NFL running backs, receivers, and tight ends are largely of the African-American Persuasion?

50. *Sports-Why is it that* during most recreational basketball games, most African-American male participants become overly aggressive and sensitive when experiencing a foul or a call with which they disagree? This display of physical and verbal aggression is exacerbated by minuscule actions which sometimes explode into avoidable physical altercations.

51. *Sports-Why is it that* the majority of the interviewees expressed that once African-American male athletes engage in improper activities, display inappropriate, unsportsmanlike conduct, or participate in actions that are deemed incomprehensively immoral, most persons of the Caucasian Persuasion label them as 'thugs?" Conversely, when the same or a similar scenario involves a Caucasian male athlete, he is rarely described as a "thug." Has the frequent use of the word "thug" in many rap artists' music (many define themselves as thugs) amplified the prevailing mindset and cleared the way for said label designation of African-American males?

52. *Sports-Why is it that* the majority of the interviewees expressed that over 30 percent of African-Americans cannot swim or are afraid to or have not learned the importance of swimming to preserve life in event a circumstance warrants the absolute

need to save a life or their own as compared to those of the Caucasian Persuasion?

53. ***Sports-Why is it that*** the majority of the interviewees expressed that since 1920 the NFL's inaugural championship, the league still has less than a third (approximately 10 of 32 teams) of African-American starting quarterbacks whereas the league's share of African-Americans players is approximately 66 percent?

54. ***Sports-Why is it that*** the majority of the interviewees expressed that they are alarmed that approximately 60 percent of NBA athletes file for bankruptcy after four to five years of retirement, and approximately 79 percent NFL athletes files for bankruptcy after two to three years after retirement and the majority are male persons of the African-American Persuasion?

55. ***Sports-Why is it that*** the majority of the interviewees expressed that they are puzzled by the commentary description of Caucasian American collegiate and NFL quarterbacks performances as "smart" or "he executed with precision," whereas African-American quarterbacks are described as "athletic or agile" when successfully accomplishing a play, milestone, or victory?

56. ***Sports-Why is it that*** most of the interviewees expressed that elitist sports which are primarily dominated and played only by persons of the Caucasian Persuasion are sports that require wealth, (i.e., polo, horse racing, sailing, tennis, squash, crew, lacrosse, equestrian, and jai alai)? The interviewees also expressed and believed that the only factor that limits persons of the African-American Persuasion from participating is the dollar and the wealthy are jubilant of said factor.

57. ***Sports-Why is it that*** the majority of the interviewees believed Caucasian male athletes are more inclined to establish an inseparable and stronger rapport with their fellow Caucasian male athletes teammates than most male African-American athletes do with their fellow male African-American teammates?

58. ***Sports-Why is it that*** the majority of the interviewees expressed that female persons of the Caucasian Persuasion are the predominant ethnic group that participate in collegiate sports like softball, swimming, golf, tennis, volleyball, soccer, gymnastics, pole-vaulting, and cross country and are consistently celebrated for their talent and winning track records on both HBCUs and PWIs campuses? Interviewees further observed that most female persons of the African-American Persuasion are celebrated but in predominantly track and field and basketball on both campuses as well.

59. ***Sports-Why is it that*** most of the interviewees of the Caucasian Persuasion are perplexed over the notion that there has not been a major increase (via media) of African-American females on the professional tennis tours? With the remarkable and exceptional rise of Venus and Serena Williams within the women professional circuit, they expressed with reluctance their interest in seeing more talented African-American females in the sport even if it undergoes a potential U. S. ethnic transformation.

60. ***Sports-Why is it that*** most of the female interviewees of the Caucasian Persuasion expressed that in the competitive world of professional women tennis, power, agility, speed, and sexy (as demonstrated by tennis greats Venice and Serena Williams) have taken the place of daintiness, gentleness, refine, and fragile? However, they are in awe of its evolution and find it difficult to compete?

Chapter 7
Sex

Sex

Sex is possibly the explicit subject that entices the human inquisitiveness in us and may be one of the most intriguing chapters in my book. We have been inundated with countless movies, television hours, weekly magazines, and other periodicals of endless myths and spot-on interpretations about sex. The consumer's acceptance and appetite for sexual exploits are increasing exponentially. The beliefs of detailed innuendos amid the African-American and Caucasian American ethnicities have consistently raised curiosity. When some of these observations and beliefs impact our lives on daily bases, a healthy dynamic is in play. We often wonder why sex is deemed the source of our mental paralysis and frequent susceptibility to psychological and physical stimuli. Other elements in society spark elevated interest and provoke stimuli, but sex produces an entirely different energy and ravenous exposure. When some think of sex, they equate it with erotica. Erotica is the stimuli that promote sexual desires and commonly accentuates potential sexual pleasures. Most of the interviewees were familiar with erotica and the exotic. Their interpretation and definition of erotica varied. But their interpretation and definition of exotic were pointed and centered on a particular ethnicity, the African-American woman.

This chapter will attempt to share observations and experiences of interviewees of both the African-American and Caucasian American Persuasions on the subject of sex. The interviewees have graciously provided their beliefs and curiosities about each other's ethnicity. Their initial reluctance caused me great concern to the point of questioning my plans to write on the subject, but when I shared my observations, they began to let their guards totally down and divulged real personal experiences and observations that were bottled up for years. When they began to expound on sex they did so with deeply expressed emotions and enthusiasm. I was startled by a few interviewees on their actual confessions on several subtopics, but prayerfully, I didn't receive or hear any experiences that would warrant the summons of arresting authorities. Their honesty coupled with their sincerity was welcoming. Admittedly, some of the interviewee's depiction of sex rendered many nuances of their ethnic exposure and experiences.

This chapter offers a plethora of interesting observations and inquiries accurately aligned with African-Americans and Caucasian Americans. Some inquiries may have surfaced periodically with robust dialogue while others may seem relatively new and encourage moderate to intense curiosity. Whatever the case, I hope this chapter will deepen your understanding of insightful differences and idiosyncrasies of those of the African-American and Caucasian Persuasions. The listing of inquiries is not intended to infer or suggest that any one ethnic group's observations are favorably elevated or unflatteringly marginalized. My views in addition to the interviewees' interpretations and experiences are neither defined as positive or negative, "it is what it is." These are the majority of interviewees and my observations.

Sex Observations / Differences

OMG

1. ***Sex-Why is it that*** the majority of the interviewees expressed that most male and female persons of the Caucasian Persuasion between the ages of 18 to 75 years old are more comfortable and more probable to expose their nude bodies publicly than most male and female persons of the African-American Persuasion in the same age bracket?

2. ***Sex-Why is it that*** the majority of the interviewees expressed that most male and female persons of the Caucasian Persuasion are more likely to deem themselves as "exhibitionists" more so than persons of the African-American Persuasion?

3. ***Sex-Why is it that*** the majority of the interviewees expressed that most male and female persons of the Caucasian Persuasion are more comfortable and more likely to attend or become members of nudist camps than male and female persons of the African-American Persuasion?

4. ***Sex-Why is it that*** the majority of the interviewees expressed that persons of the Caucasian Persuasion have a tendency to indulge or participate in extraordinary or extreme sex acts, (i.e., masochism, bestiality, diaper pail sessions, and fisting) considerably more than persons of the African-American Persuasion?

5. ***Sex-Why is it that*** the majority of the interviewees expressed that most male and female persons of the Caucasian Persuasion who are tanned, shapely, barely clothed, and who display physical frontal imprints, (i.e., nipples and genitalia bulge), particularly at pool sides and beaches are considered provocative, sexually

risqué but appealing, seductive, and sensuous? Frequent observances reveal that persons of the African-American Persuasion who are naturally tanned, shapely, barely clothed, and display the same physical frontal imprints are considered obscene, vulgar, despicable, perverted, and repugnant.

6. *Sex-Why is it that* the majority of the interviewees expressed that most male persons of the Caucasian Persuasion in the lower economic, social class tend to be more homophobic and inclined to cause physical harm to gays than the average male of the African-American Persuasion in the same economic class?

7. *Sex-Why is it that* the majority of the interviewees expressed that most female persons of the African-American Persuasion say that penis size matters and place more emphases on length and girth? Interviewees further exposed that most female persons of the Caucasian Persuasion say that penis size does not matter and they place less emphasis on the physical composition.

8. *Sex-Why is it that* the majority of the interviewees expressed that most female persons of the African-American Persuasion who happen to be exotic dancers are more likely to exercise the practice of "butt clapping" and "twerking," full vaginal exposure in the presence of predominantly males of the African-American Persuasion but forego such performances in the presence of mostly males of the Caucasian Persuasion?

9. *Sex-Why is it that* the majority of the interviewees expressed that most young to middle aged (20 to 45 years) male persons of the Caucasian Persuasion quietly express deep and painful ethnic fears of the thought of their ex-girlfriend or significant other having a sexual relationship with a male person of the

African-American Persuasion that fits the description tall, dark, and handsome?

10. *Sex-Why is it that* the majority of the interviewees expressed that most younger male persons of the Caucasian Persuasion between the ages of 20-30 years old who have girlfriends or even wives are more willing and desirous with heightened curiosity to experience the sexual act of a "threesome" with a male person of the African-American Persuasion who is endowed tall, dark, and handsome than with males of the Caucasian Persuasion?

11. *Sex-Why is it that* the majority of the interviewees expressed that most males of the Caucasian Persuasion are more attracted to and place more emphases on women's legs and breasts than any other body features? More frequently, most males of the African-American Persuasion are attracted to and put more emphasis on women having a noticeable and shapely butt than any other characteristic.

12. *Sex-Why is it that* the majority of the interviewees expressed that most female persons of the Caucasian Persuasion, who reside in the upper social-economic class, who have an attraction for or have sexual relations with an African-American male, consider these acts as experiences of "exotica" or "jungle fever" rather than confessing to their longing to test the myth of the "African-American male's sexual euphoria?"

13. *Sex-Why is it that* the majority of the interviewees expressed that most young male and female persons of the Caucasian Persuasion during the winter season begin to unclothe immediately or expose all of their upper body or become partially nude once exterior temperatures rise to at least 65 degrees? They enjoy the freedom of partial nudity more so than persons of the African-American Persuasion.

14. ***Sex-Why is it that*** the majority of the African-American and Caucasian American interviewees equally expressed that more females of both persuasions who were closet lesbians are coming out more and amplifying their masculine disposition by wearing extremely short hair, baggy pants, extra large shirts, little to no make-up, and projecting manly body gestures and movements?

15. ***Sex-Why is it that*** the majority of the interviewees expressed that most male persons of the African-American Persuasion with bald/cleanly shaved heads are quietly deemed attractive, highly exotic, and sexier than bald/cleanly shaved headed male persons of the Caucasian Persuasion?

16. ***Sex-Why is it that*** most of the interviewees expressed that today's pop culture, which is mainly comprised of male and female persons of the Caucasian Persuasion, defines exclusively and unfalteringly female persons of the Caucasian Persuasion as the sexiest, hottest, and most beautiful women in the world?

17. ***Sex-Why is it that*** most of the interviewees expressed that females of the Caucasian Persuasion concisely and explicitly voice their desires to be romanced by a male who is tall, dark and handsome? Their depiction of such a man is naturally an African-American or male of color, but they will vehemently deny such description and feverishly defend their perfect male specimen as one only of the Caucasian Persuasion.

18. ***Sex-Why is it that*** most of the interviewees expressed that most male and female comedians of the African-American Persuasion consistently center their acts around or emphasize comedic subjects such as oral sex, sexual positions (doggy style), penis size, and genital hygiene? Frequent observances reveal that most male and female comedians of the Caucasian Persuasion seldom speak on such subjects.

19. ***Sex-Why is it that*** most of the interviewees expressed that most females of both African-American and Caucasian Persuasions assume that the trendy prophylactic "Magnums" were inevitably created and prescribed purposefully for the African-American male than for the Caucasian male?

20. ***Sex-Why is it that*** most of the interviewees expressed that most males of both the African-American Persuasion and Caucasian Persuasion frequently speak about fantasies of making love to females of both the African-American Persuasion and Caucasian Persuasion but rarely hear of African-American females frequently speaking about fantasies of making love to males of the Caucasian Persuasion?

21. ***Sex-Why is it that*** most of the interviewees expressed that the majority of adult films feature mainly persons of the Caucasian Persuasion when societal opinions invariably reference African-Americans as significant sexual stimuli?

22. ***Sex-Why is it that*** most of the interviewees expressed that male and female persons of the Caucasian Persuasion are more susceptible and desirous to receive upper and lower body piercing, (i.e., nose, eyelids, lips, ears, tongue, nipples, penis, and clitoris), than persons of the African-American Persuasion?

23. ***Sex-Why is it that*** most females interviewees of the African-American Persuasion expressed that most noted fashion designers of the Caucasian Persuasion who hire male runway models rarely provide opportunities for African-American male models even when the fashion industry consistently reveals that attractive male African-American models who are of medium to dark complexion are more exotic and sexier than Caucasian male models?

24. ***Sex-Why is it that*** most of the interviewees expressed that most African-American males are more likely not to don sports swim wear such as bikini Speedos at private, public pools or beaches? Conversely, male persons of the Caucasian Persuasion are more inclined to do so.

25. ***Sex-Why is it that*** most of the interviewees expressed that primarily persons of the Caucasian Persuasion practice partner swapping and participate in voyeuristic activities that include husbands, wives, boyfriends, and girlfriends substantially more so than persons of the African-American Persuasion?

26. ***Sex-Why is it that*** most of the interviewees expressed that in present day culture, African-American males and females between the ages 20 - 35 years old have been defined as sexually provocative, entertaining, arousing, stimulating, promiscuous, lascivious, physically endowed and impressive, but the standard motion picture and porn industry overwhelmingly features more persons of the Caucasian Persuasion who do not fit or have the aforementioned attributes?

27. ***Sex-Why is it that*** most of the interviewees expressed that most male persons of the African-American Persuasion embrace the genitalia myth that they are the most physically endowed males of most ethnic groups? They also believe metaphorically, that the perpetuation of said narrative affords them one of the powerful intimidation factors to debase primarily male persons of the Caucasian Persuasion?

28. ***Sex-Why is it that*** most of the interviewees expressed that most male persons of the African-American Persuasion who indulge in several homosexual acts while married ("the down low") do not define themselves as homosexuals or bisexuals but believe it is a natural desire to experiment with the same sex? Conversely, most male persons of the Caucasian Persuasion

who indulge in the same activities are more inclined to accept their status as a homosexual or bisexual and will depart from their marital status at a faster rate than most African-American males.

29. **Sex-Why is it that** most of the interviewees expressed that male persons of the Caucasian Persuasion are more desirous to receive or experience penis enlargements via personal penis enlargement pumps, pills, or surgical enlargements than male persons of the African-American Persuasion?

30. **Sex-Why is it that** most of the interviewees expressed that most males of the African-American Persuasion who happen to be comedians approach the subject of oral sex with alacrity and intensity more so than they did five to ten years ago? Interviewees advanced the notion that most males of the Caucasian Persuasion, who happen to be comedians rarely address the subject of oral sex.

31. **Sex-Why is it that** most of the interviewees expressed that most female persons of the Caucasian Persuasion who happen to be exotic dancers introduce props as a part of their dance routine, while female persons of the African-American Persuasion who are exotic dancers rarely draw upon props to accent or enhance their stage performance, but dance more explicitly?

32. **Sex-Why is it that** most of the interviewees expressed that most male persons of the African-American Persuasion who happen to be exotic dancers emphasize or highlight their endowment first, and then focus on their muscular toned physiques, while the Caucasian exotic dancers do the reverse by emphasizing their muscular toned physiques first, and then their endowment?

33. **Sex-Why is it that** most of the interviewees expressed that most male persons of the African-American Persuasion who

happen to be exotic dancers fully uncover themselves, display their endowment, and initiate direct audience participation in a setting where the majority participants are female persons of the African-American Persuasion? Further, the same exotic dancers' opportunities for full exposure are more reserved, and the unveiling of their endowment is curtailed substantially when the majority of audience participants are female persons of the Caucasian Persuasion?

34. ***Sex-Why is it that*** most of the interviewees expressed that most female star actresses of the Caucasian Persuasion who participate in the pornography industry are paid more than the African-American female and male pornography stars when the objective and the line of work is virtually identical?

35. ***Sex-Why is it that*** most of the interviewees expressed that most female persons of the African-American Persuasion who participate in the sex for fee industry dub themselves as "street hoes" and "tricks," but most persons of the Caucasian Persuasion glamorize the act of prostitution and dub themselves as "ladies of the evening," or "upscale call girls," or "female escorts?"

Yes, This Is The Deal

36. ***Sex-Why is it that*** most of the interviewees expressed that when male persons of the African-American Persuasion who know the risks of participating in consensual sexual relations with a female of Caucasian Persuasion still fall prey to rape charges? The Caucasian female can, will, and has accused the African-American male of rape, and the social order will accept as true and embrace her victimization status swiftly regardless of the lack of physical evidence.

37. *Sex-Why is it that* most of the interviewees expressed that most male persons of the Caucasian Persuasion express more verbal excitement and become aggressively aroused when being entertained by a Caucasian female exotic dancer with excessively large breasts? Conversely, the male persons of the African-American Persuasion express marginal excitement and do not become aggressively aroused by Caucasian females with excessively large breasts.

38. *Sex-Why is it that* most of the interviewees expressed that a male person of the African-American Persuasion who has participated in multiple adult films has not been annotated with the legendary status as that of the late John Holmes, especially when historical myths and expressions of today's pop culture equates sexual endowment with the male person of the African-American Persuasion? What male person of the African-American Persuasion has the industry celebrated with such universal status?

39. *Sex-Why is it that* the majority of the interviewees expressed that most males of the Caucasian Persuasion are acutely more attracted to female persons of both African-American and Caucasian Persuasions that are described as a size 2, 4, or 6 more so than most males of the African-American Persuasion. Most African-American males have a yearning for females of both persuasions that are described as a size 6, 8, 10, or greater, they express with candor "more meat on the bones is more loving to hold."

40. *Sex-Why is it that* most of the females interviewees expressed that most males of the African-American Persuasion define well endowed (at full erection) as being equipped with a minimum of a 6-inch circumference/girth and 8 inches in length?

41. **Sex-Why is it that** most of the females interviewees expressed that most males of the Caucasian Persuasion define well endowed (at full erection) as being equipped with a minimum of a 5 1/2-inch circumference/girth and 6 1/2 inches in length?

42. **Sex-Why is it that** most of the Caucasians interviewees expressed that past cable television monthly special series such as *HBO's Real Sex and Taxi Cab Confessions* depict persons of the Caucasian Persuasion as ones who prefer and participate in extremely unusual sexual activities more so than persons of the African-American Persuasion?

43. **Sex-Why is it that** most of the interviewees expressed that most male persons of the African-American Persuasion in the age bracket of approximately 18 - 35 years of age believe that they have to shield the historical reputation or myth of the African-American genital endowment in any conversation centered on sexuality or sexual endurance? Additionally, why is it that most males of said persuasion who deem themselves, or consider themselves endowed are most often lean or slim in stature. Most male persons of the Caucasian Persuasion rarely extend such definitive discourse.

44. **Sex-Why is it that** most of the interviewees expressed that most male exotic dancers of the African-American Persuasion are expected (by the industry and African-American female fans) to have an extremely "cut" physique and a minimum relaxed or flaccid genital endowment of a 7-inch penis? The same inflexible expectation or standard is not required of the male exotic dancers of the Caucasian Persuasion.

45. **Sex-Why is it that** most of the interviewees expressed that most persons of the Caucasian Persuasion are more inclined, recognized, and celebrated not to wear underwear, (i.e., male boxer shorts, briefs or female panties)? Conversely, persons of

the African-American Persuasion are more likely to wear the above undergarments.

46. ***Sex-Why is it that*** most of the interviewees expressed that female persons of the Caucasian Persuasion are more apt to participate in multiple partner sexual activities with male persons of the African-American Persuasion, while female persons of the African-American Persuasion are most unlikely to engage with multiple partners who happen to be male persons of the Caucasian Persuasion?

47. ***Sex-Why is it that*** most of the interviewees expressed that most male and female persons of the Caucasian Persuasion who are married and thirty-five years of age or older, are more inclined to discuss their sex lives, sex routines, and sex schedules openly with anyone who is willing to listen? On the contrary, married male and female persons of the African-American Persuasion who are the same age seldom discuss their sex lives openly with anyone.

48. ***Sex-Why is it that*** most of the interviewees expressed that most female persons of the Caucasian Persuasion are less aggressive or demanding to view total nudity of the African-American male exotic dancers? Interviewees further noted that most female persons of the African-American Persuasion are more aggressive, they expect and demand to see the full nudity of African-American male exotic dancers.

49. **Sex-Why is it that** most of the interviewees expressed that most male persons of the Caucasian Persuasion who are exotic dancers do not have to be well endowed, or perform as frequently to amass financial security in the exotic dancing industry? Conversely, most male persons of the African-American Persuasion are expected to be well endowed and

perform more frequently to simply gain marginal financial security.

50. **Sex-Why is it that** most of the interviewees expressed that past cable television monthly specials such as *HBO's Real Sex and Taxi Cab Confessions* cater to the exotic experiences of mostly and primarily persons of the Caucasian Persuasion? Seldom does HBO solely show footage of fetishes, sexual fantasies, or exotic experiences of persons of the African-American Persuasion.

51. **Sex-Why is it that** most of the interviewees expressed that most persons of the Caucasian Persuasion believe that if the cable industry begins showing full nudity of persons of the African-American Persuasion as consistently seen of persons of the Caucasian Persuasion, Caucasian viewers will become appalled, infuriated, protest, and anticipate sponsorships will plummet?

52. *Sex-Why is it that* most of the interviewees expressed that most female actresses of the African-American Persuasion are rarely involved in romantic relationship scenes with an African-American male that do not have strong sexual content. Conversely, female actresses of the Caucasian Persuasion frequently do and have had romantic relations in movie scenes with a Caucasian male with the absence of strong sexual content.

53. *Sex-Why is it that* most of the interviewees expressed that the adult film industry that parades most male and female persons of the Caucasian Persuasion who star/participate in contemporary chic adult films appear to be more so in better physical shape, (i.e., lean, shapely, fit, and attractive), than the few African-American stars/participants?

54. ***Sex-Why is it that*** most of the interviewees expressed that most single male persons of the Caucasian Persuasion are less bothered by what others may think or question about genuine friendly male bonding, especially when monthly or quarterly weekend excursions are scheduled, (i.e., camping trips, cycling, fishing, hunting, hiking, golfing, etc)? However, most single male persons of the African-American Persuasion are more sensitive to what others may think or say about their time with other men friends, especially African-American females. They believe African-American females will question their sexuality and assume the worst even if it is pure male friendship.

55. ***Sex-Why is it that*** most of the interviewees expressed that most female persons of the Caucasian Persuasion in the adult film industry express that they have greater vaginal sensation, will endure more pain, and are less disagreeable to partake in oral sex and with multiple partners who are African-American males? Conversely, most females of the African-American Persuasion choose not to engage in the acts as mentioned above with African-American males but will engage in said actions with male persons of the Caucasian Persuasion.

56. ***Sex-Why is it that*** nearly every one of the interviewees expressed that female persons of the Caucasian Persuasion are more likely to entertain and undergo cosmetic surgery for extreme breast enlargements than female persons of the African-American Persuasion?

57. ***Sex-Why is it that*** nearly every one of the interviewees expressed that female persons of the Caucasian Persuasion who are deemed stars in the adult film industry are elevated and celebrated substantially above female persons of the African-American Persuasion by establishing a brand that includes the production of paraphernalia and exotic toys? Additionally, what African-American females have been listed as most beautiful

and celebrated similarly as that of Jenna, Jameson, Tori Black, Gianna Michaels or Jenna Haze in the industry?

58. ***Sex-Why is it that*** nearly every one of the interviewees expressed that most male persons of the Caucasian Persuasion (heterosexual) express that their preferred sexual position with a female is the "missionary position?"

59. ***Sex-Why is it that*** nearly every one of the interviewees expressed that most male persons of the African-American Persuasion (heterosexual) express that their preferred sexual position with a female is the "doggy style?"

60. ***Sex-Why is it that*** nearly every one of the interviewees expressed that most female persons of the Caucasian Persuasion are more likely to discount or criticize the buttock protrusion of the African-American female? Non-millennials females of the Caucasian Persuasion frequently project disparaging expressions as "their butts are too big," or "that is not fashionable," or "that is disgusting."

61. ***Sex-Why is it that*** nearly every one of the interviewees expressed that most female persons of the African-American Persuasion are more likely to discount or criticize the breast enlargement of a Caucasian female? Non-millennial females of the African-American Persuasion frequently project disparaging expressions as "their breast are too big," or "that is not sexy and it should be painful," or "that is disgusting," or "totally fake," or "they should be happy with what God gave them."

62. ***Sex-Why is it that*** nearly every one of the interviewees expressed that most media driven female persons of the Caucasian Persuasion that are allied with rap, hip hop, and professional sports athletes who happen to have been graced (naturally or

cosmetically) with large buttocks are celebrated by the media and particularly African-American males? Unexpectedly, most African-American females are not as critical of the celebrated attributes, but are frustrated in that African-American males amplify the Caucasian females' buttocks endowment and side step them and crown Caucasian females as queen of sex, while the Caucasian females' celebrity appeal and notoriety go up and African-American females' celebrity appeal and notoriety go down.

63. ***Sex-Why is it that*** nearly everyone of the interviewees expressed that most male and female persons of the Caucasian Persuasion are more inclined to humiliate, bully, and destroy another person's progression in life by mercilessly and secretly recording and posting their most personal and intimate details of their sexual experiences through social media? The interviewees also noted that most persons of the African-American Persuasion rarely engage in ruthless acts relative to exposing another person's intimate sexual experiences.

64. ***Sex-Why is it that*** nearly everyone of the female interviewees of both African-American and Caucasian American Persuasions, are more attracted to and inclined with zealousness to befriend a male person of the African-American Persuasion who has curly hair, is 21 to 30 years of age, smart, lean, tall, attractive, athletic or muscular build, light or dark complexion, and reportedly endowed than a male person of the Caucasian Persuasion with similar features? However, if the Caucasian male possesses the same attributes and introduces wealth in to the equation, the appeal would shift towards the Caucasian male. Both African-American and Caucasian females expressed that sex appeal is essential, but money takes on an entirely different dynamic.

Chapter 8
Health

Health

Health impacts all human life and can be defined in simple or intricate terms. Health may encompass physical appearances, behavioral qualities, and emotional disposition. This chapter will place more emphases on physical appearances and behavioral qualities and pass over emotional disposition because said definition can take on an entirely different dynamic and can be difficult to observe. One's emotional disposition may summon more subjectivity than objectivity. As mentioned, physical and behavioral components are the focus of this chapter highlighting African-Americans and Caucasian Americans accessibility to healthy foods, comprehensive education to good health, and health disparities. My annotations, the interviewees' observations, and interpretations are from a non-academic position. Our inquiries were formed and generated from consistent personal experiences or observations of both ethnicities.

The health industry is an enormous and multifarious instrument in the orchestra of life and humanity. It has sizeable amounts of intricately structured layers of policies and procedures, not to mention individual and organizational responsibilities. It is a community of corporations, doctors, lawyers, nurses, medical and equipment specialists, patients, pharmaceutical and equipment reps, state and federal government, and financial institutions. It is a massive economic engine in any community. This is where the interviewees elevated the subtle, and in some cases, uncovered blatant disparities between African-Americans and Caucasian Americans. Accessibility is a major hindrance to quality and preventive health primarily in the African-American community. The interviewees have shared significant but interesting views that suggest the absolute need to reform the healthcare system. They have also observed that sufficient means (money) plainly allow persons of

African-American or Caucasian Persuasion to have suitable access to health care. One may conclude that money perhaps is the purest approach to access good health care.

Money is the essential necessity to access and have quality healthcare to help maintain healthy living, but there are other contributing factors that are essential as well. The interviewees and I have observed and questioned other essential factors that support and enhance healthy living such as education, physical exercise, and common judgment. The aforementioned supports and enhancements have their place in healthy living when knowing one's numbers, when and how to exercise, and dietary nutritional consumption. This chapter not only questions a series of interests in which persons of the African-American and Caucasian Persuasions indulge or impact their health, but the interviewees and I included other noticeable health differences between the two ethnic groups. These are the majority of interviewees and my observations.

Health Observations / Differences

This Is Unbelievable

1. ***Health-Why is it that*** most of the interviewees expressed that most persons of the African-American Persuasion choose not to alter voluntarily their eating habits and intake of numerous types of food that have been determined to increase the threat of diabetes, cancer, hypertension, and acute heart failure?

2. ***Health-Why is it that*** most of the interviewees expressed that most male persons of the African-American Persuasion rarely schedule annual physicals or health screenings?

3. ***Health-Why is it that*** most of the interviewees revealed that most persons of the Caucasian Persuasion understand the health risks of smoking, but are more inclined to smoke heavily and frequently in work areas that permit such activity?

4. ***Health-Why is it that*** most of the interviewees expressed that most persons of the Caucasian Persuasion are given more leniency to take a break or a day off than persons of the African-American Persuasion concerning their work productivity when they have health conditions that are not life-threatening, (i.e., headaches, sinus irritations, back pain, a mental health day, and carpal tunnel pain)?

5. ***Health-Why is it that*** most of the interviewees expressed that most female persons of the Caucasian Persuasion continually seek any form of medication to solve all of their problems and desired physical results?

6. ***Health-Why is it that*** the health service community consistently forewarns male persons of the African-American Persuasion

of the danger and potential health risks of fatty foods, lack of frequent exercise, and the need to have annual health screening, but African- American males invariably fall victim to increased heart disease, hypertension, prostate cancer, and other preventable and treatable illnesses?

7. *Health-Why is it that* the health service community consistently forewarns female persons of the African-American Persuasion of the need to get regular breast examinations possibly to identify the early signs of breast cancer, but the African-American female invariably falls victim to increased cases of breast cancer more so than female persons of the Caucasian Persuasion?

8. *Health-Why is it that* most of the interviewees expressed that most professional male persons of the African-American Persuasion exhibit poor fingernail and toenail care in comparison to most professional male persons of the Caucasian Persuasion?

9. *Health-Why is it that* most of the interviewees expressed that most female persons of the African American Persuasion rarely visit their gynecologist annually or every eighteen months? Conversely, most female persons of the Caucasian Persuasion visit their gynecologist regularly.

10. *Health-Why is it that* most of the interviewees expressed that most male and female persons of the African American Persuasion find it extremely difficult to participate in research programs which address medical conditions that primarily, solely, and severely affect their ethnic gene pool, (i.e., sickle cell, diabetes, kidney disease, heart disease, breast cancer, prostate cancer, and colon cancer)?

11. *Health-Why is it that* most of the interviewees expressed that
     most male persons of the African-American Persuasion rarely
     schedule annual physical exams or health screenings and are
     more susceptible to extensive or severe sexually transmitted
     diseases (STDs)? Why do young African-Americans allow
     mythical sexual designations (endowment) dictate the absence
     of the use of condoms and convince their female partner to
     receive "The Real McCoy" and natural sensation instead of
     full protection?

12. *Health-Why is it that* most of the interviewees expressed
     that most male persons of the African American Persuasion
     genuinely believe that a female who is his girlfriend, fiancé, or
     wife is no longer a woman after a hysterectomy whether they
     wished to have children or not?

13. *Health-Why is it that* most of the interviewees expressed that
     most persons of the Caucasian Persuasion shampoo their hair at
     least twice a week while most persons of the African-American
     Persuasion wash their hair at least or not more than once a week?

14. *Health-Why is it that* most of the interviewees expressed that
     persons of the Caucasian Persuasion are more inclined to allow
     their child or children to walk in public areas without shoes or
     socks exposing the feet to a number of bacteria and potential
     cuts?

15. *Health-Why is it that* more persons of the Caucasian Persuasion
     enter the health care field more so than persons of the African-
     American Persuasion when demographics indicate a shortage
     of medical doctors and nurses in rural predominantly African-
     American communities?

16. *Health-Why is it that* nearly all of the interviewees expressed
     that most persons of the Caucasian Persuasion are more

inclined to publicly expose with comfort an open wound, cut, and surgical stitches more so than persons of the African-American Persuasion?

17. ***Health-Why is it that*** nearly all of the interviewees expressed that most persons of the Caucasian Persuasion are received with open arms more so than persons of the African-American Persuasion when the media exposes the birth of, or separation of Siamese twins?

18. ***Health-Why is it that*** nearly all of the interviewees expressed that most persons of the African-American Persuasion have a tendency not to ask questions about the procedure or medication prescribed during office visits? Conversely, most persons of the Caucasian Persuasion ask multiple questions regarding any office procedure and medication prescribed during office visits.

19. ***Health-Why is it that*** nearly all of the interviewees expressed that most male persons of the African-American Persuasion are more reluctant to allow male doctors to perform full physical examinations than most male persons of the Caucasian Persuasion?

20. ***Health-Why is it that*** nearly all of the interviewees expressed that persons of the African-American Persuasion make up less than six percent of all doctors in the United States? If more African-American doctors were in population, especially in the African-American communities, would it not significantly improve the health related issues that are increasingly prevalent in said communities?

21. ***Health-Why is it that*** nearly all of the interviewees expressed that persons of the African-American Persuasion make up less than two percent of all healthcare related equipment suppliers, equipment sales representatives, and the pharmaceutical sales

industry? Why is it that most African-Americans who have considered said fields have been told that the prerequisites include a bachelor's degree and medical sales experience? However, most persons of the Caucasian Persuasion who enter said field may not have either.

22. *Health-Why is it that* nearly all of the interviewees expressed that persons of the African-American Persuasion who require emergency medical attention, especially young African-American males, are mainly transported and treated for stabbings or gunshot wounds? Young male persons of the Caucasian Persuasion are mainly transported and treated for broken bones, deep cuts from skateboard falls, hiking missteps, car wrecks, and prank mishaps.

23. *Health-Why is it that* nearly all of the interviewees expressed that most persons of the Caucasian Persuasion insist on acquiring golden tans via laying out capturing sun rays and visits to tanning salons when overwhelming evidence concludes that excessive ultraviolet rays are a leading contributor to skin cancer (melanoma)?

24. *Health-Why is it that* nearly all of the interviewees expressed that persons of the African-American Persuasion are more inclined to overcook vegetables depleting all nutritional values?

25. *Health-Why is it that* almost all of the interviewees expressed that persons of the African-American Persuasion are more prone to over-season foods with sodium and add excessive sweeteners to beverages, (i.e., tea, lemonade, and Kool-Aid)?

26. *Health-Why is it that* nearly all of the interviewees expressed that persons of the African-American Persuasion are more inclined to cook and ingest fried pork, chicken, and fish, than baked meats?

27. ***Health-Why is it that*** nearly all of the interviewees expressed that a growing number of young children of the African-American Persuasion are obese and not being taken seriously in regards to initiating sustainable preventive measures to thwart potential future health problems caused by their obesity?

28. ***Health-Why is it that*** nearly all of the interviewees expressed that the death rate among middle-aged Caucasian males is increasing substantially? Some suggest that the increase is due to financial strains, work once secured by non-college educated Caucasian males, (i.e., manufacturing and construction jobs) is evaporating rapidly, and pension/retirement bankruptcy are compelling them to cope with the aid of alcohol, heroin, and opioid drugs.

29. ***Health-Why is it that*** nearly all of the interviewees expressed that the death rate among young African-American males between 15-34 years of age is homicide whereas the death rate among young Caucasian males of the same age is accidental death?

30. ***Health-Why is it that*** nearly all of the interviewees expressed that when a health crisis emerges which impacts mostly persons of the African-American Persuasion, slow action or mitigation efforts are always predictable? Conversely, when a health crisis emerges that impacts persons of the Caucasian Persuasion, the gauntlet is let down to foil its expansion with expediency.

Afterword

I hope that you were enlightened by my observations which consist of distinct behaviors of people of both ethnic persuasions. One may define the aforementioned learned behaviors as the result of cultural exposure. However, what I have also discerned during my observations and communications with numerous individuals and diverse groups of both ethnicities is that they frequently and emphatically depict the different ethnic idiosyncrasies as culturally based. Are we not products of our individual environments but coexisting in one culture, (i.e., the American culture)? Understandably, there are pockets of subcultures under the big umbrella of the American culture, but I am of the opinion that both African-Americans and Caucasian Americans are invariably disconnected.

Take, for example, most persons of the African-American Persuasion expressed that when President Donald J. Trump (a Caucasian male) is permitted to consistently sneer African-Americans and purposely dismantle and destroy the delicate tattered fabric of improved racial harmony, will he be held accountable. They stated that they know his actions are done to stimulate his alarming narcissism but challenge why the absence of persons of the Caucasian Persuasion public, relentless, and potent storming denouncement. Most persons of the African-American Persuasion are acutely cognizant of the potential of history repeating itself especially when political measures are introduced similar to a "Jim Crow" society and targets their communities most egregiously. Racial tension is dangerously heightening. Most persons of the Caucasian Persuasion self-confessed that if President Barack Obama (an African-American male), conducted himself in a similar matter and used the "bully pulpit" to elevate and incite racial tensions as the present President Trump, they would take matters into their own hands to remove him from office. In doing so, violence perhaps would have been introduced to thwart African-Americans aggression.

Most Caucasians unenthusiastically stated that yes, there are double standards and consequences for persons of the Caucasian Persuasion and persons of the African-American Persuasion. It is unfortunate but "it is what it is." Is racial unity attainable? I contend that it is.

Ethnic solidarity presents itself only when a national crisis emerges. Anytime after that, heightened levels of ethnic acceptance, tolerance, and benevolence are short lived. Each group goes back to its same mode of operation.

Both ethnic groups rarely coexist harmoniously. Wait, before you veer to the left or right of my statement. What I have noticed and observed is that both ethnic groups do not attempt to understand each other unless forced to do so, either through legislation, or political posturing. I believe if both groups unpeel a thin layer of learned pretentiousness, especially in the areas of business, politics, education, health, and fashion, the level of trust, prosperity, and shared values will increase.

I am not advocating that both groups relinquish their heritage or acquiesce to the other group's beliefs or approach to everyday living. My inference is simple: acknowledge each other's differences, encourage openness, remove barriers, embrace the positives, mitigate the negative, and promote God's interest, and not just your own group's interest. It is my understanding through simple life experiences that both ethnic groups desire the same out of life. Persons in both groups are desirous for peace, opportunity, love, and a better future for their offspring.

Regardless of our interests, we are first children of God. We did not birth ourselves. We all have red blood running through our veins. We all require oxygen, food, and water to sustain life. We are born with unlocked minds (observe children 1 year to 2 years old playing with each other free from learned ethnic prejudices and behavior). We do not hire ourselves, as individuals: we do not print our currency; we do not turn on or off our daily primary source of energy—the sun, and we do not determine emphatically our life plan or life expectancy at birth. Thus, one's self-righteous, propensity to demean, obsession with greed, and calculated acts that thwart other ethnic groups' positive progression are destructive and irreverent.

If we are not in control of the few matters as mentioned above, then who are we to question God's work and dismiss others? I believe we should exert the smallest effort to attempt to understand our differences, consider an adjustment of the heart, and yield to do what is right because neither ethnic group is going anywhere soon.

These are the 3,200 plus interviewees and my observations. What are yours?

Unvoiced Sentiments and Perceptions

Why is it that most male interviewees of the Caucasian Persuasion expressed that they have observed and believe that male persons of the African-American Persuasion have had historically significant challenges and issues for which they did not contribute to and were emphatically above suspicion for their disparities? Moreover, they believed African-American males were entirely and solely responsible for their past and current financial, social, employment, health, political, and educational gaps between the two ethnic groups. However, most of the interviewees (some reluctantly and with apprehension) expressed that they believed that if African-American males manage their outside of community spending, pool their financial resources to purchase and own property, boldly enforce the importance of education, mentor to their youth especially their males, and fully support each other, fiscal and political disparities would be greatly minimized.

Also, why is it that most male interviewees of the Caucasian Persuasion have an in-depth disdain for male persons of the African-American Persuasion? Most male interviewees of the Caucasian Persuasion differentiated their unintentional and stanch loathing of male persons of the African-American Persuasion by expressing their ill-at-ease with them in primarily community and social settings. However, their most disparaging charges against the African-American male were the audacity for their communities to be self-sustaining void of any need for financial or political support from Caucasian influence. Most male persons of the Caucasian Persuasion expressed that they would be extremely nervous if they were not in position to confirm or deny financial gains of the African-American male. Financial, educational, and political control are paramount to maintain the advantage over them. Surprisingly, most Caucasian male interviewees were not particular fearful of organized African-American gangs. Their absence of fear intrinsically is that they don't have to reside in the same community. Their communities are usually greater than ten miles apart and most gang members do not travel as a group into their communities. They believe that they will more than likely have the judicial arm of government on their side because most top positions in said arena are held by people that look like them.

The male Caucasian interviewees further noted that most African-American gangs destroy themselves and their communities. They continued to articulate that the African-American gangs do not control financial institutions or well-organized revenue generating enterprises. Their structure is limited to third and fourth tier drug distribution. The older interviewees have not witnessed in the past 30 years any form of changes in the African-American gang's recruitment, legitimate entrepreneurship, or financial protection of their communities to insure the dollar circulates at least ten times as comparison to one time. Exercising the frequent retaliation tactic as a drive-by shooting is spineless and ignorant which is repeated over and over. Older interviewees continued to express that African-American males can't blame them for causing the killing of each other day-in and day-out. Are the killings protecting multi-million-dollar initiatives (i.e., health care facilities, new schools, STEM programs, construction of parks, multiple community job opportunities, college academic scholarships, etc.) or is it over a $200 drug deal gone awry? Where is the logic? Many stated that if the killings stay in their communities, "have at it."

Below are a few of the interviewee's undisguised potent dissection and presuppositions of male persons of the African-American Persuasion.

Their neighbors don't respect them.
Their families don't revere them.
Their communities don't respect them.
They don't respect each other.
They don't respect themselves.
They don't trust each other.

They don't work together.
They don't love each other.
They don't depend on each other.
They don't invest in or with each other.
They don't lift each other.
They don't pool their resources.
They don't mentor each other.
They don't own anything.
They don't educate each other.
They don't stand together.
They don't respect their women.
They seem to abhor our existence and views on telling
them to pull up their boot straps to negate poverty.
They are exceptionally creative, smart, resilient, and talented.
They don't build wealth.
They don't protect each other or their communities.
They don't value property/real estate.
They consume everything "stuff" that has no real value.
They cheat and steal from each other.
They are physically intimidating.
They pull down each other.
They senselessly kill each other.
They have pronounced sculpture physiques
They have an attraction to jewelry, clothes,
and are sexually prowess.
They have an affinity for particular canines in
the terrier and large working groups.

Why is it that most male interviewees of the African-American Persuasion have an exhaustive disdain for male persons of the Caucasian Persuasion? Many male interviewees of the Caucasian Persuasion expressed that their little experience working with nonprofessional and professional African-American males have been relatively positive. They are hard workers and don't complain about any and everything especially as subordinates. Most African-American males vehemently believe Caucasian males persistently design, in most scenarios, clandestine political ploys that restrict their financial advancement or political influence. They believe that they determinedly marginalize their ancestry importance, contributions, and resilience.

When a group of African-American athletes, musicians, actors or political commentators exercise their constitutional first amendment, freedom of speech when members of their ethnicity fall prey to frequent out-of-control police aggression or death, they are immediately portrayed as radicals, unpatriotic, and ingrates. Their patriotism becomes the subject matter and is frequently tested. Their means of earning a living is not earned. It is given to them (a handout). Their income is viscerally questioned, their behavior is cyclical and will never alter, and they should be grateful that Caucasian Americans allowed them to freely partake in private or corporate owned sports, music, or multi-million-dollar film enterprises.

Also, why is it that most male interviewees of the African-American Persuasion expressed that they have observed and believe that most male persons of the Caucasian Persuasion are resentfully cognizant and abhor the ethnic population shift that they intensely want to control and eliminate? They also believe that most Caucasian males have sustained their aggressive hold on financial, educational, judicial, medical, and political institutions. While maintaining their hold, the interviewees consistently questioned why most male persons of the Caucasian foster greediness, a xenophobic state of mind, the obsessive intoxication of power, and maliciousness? Below are a few of the interviewee's further gut-wrenching views, opinions, and perceptions of male persons of the Caucasian Persuasion.

They don't do business with people that don't look like them.
They don't associate with people that don't look like them.
They don't introduce or convey positive images
and messages of other ethnic groups.
They don't live in other people's communities.
They don't enjoy worshiping with other ethnic groups.
They don't respect their women.
They don't acknowledge empathy for the poor.
They don't have empathy or respect for the poor.
They don't believe they are privileged.
They don't care to understand other ethnic group's values.
They don't acknowledge their greed mentality.
They don't respect another ethnic groups' authority.
They don't respect another ethnic groups' leadership.
They own everything.
They create policies that advance only their
desires to become powerful and wealthy.
They cheat and steal to advance themselves.
They believe they know what is best for everyone.
They enjoy spending money to acquire fine
wines, lavish homes, and foreign travel.
They fear other people with authority.
They thrive on diluting the influence of others.
They thrive on creating policies of exclusion and separatism.
They consistently cheat and lie to be in leadership positions.
They marginalize hard work of others.
They know how to maintain their wealth for generations.
They have to control everything regardless
of their educational level.
They are lazy, fragile, and acute gun enthusiasts.
They are fearful and angry.
They revere violence and are malicious.
They take care of people that look like them.
They are destructive.

Why is it that most female interviewees of the Caucasian Persuasion expressed that they have observed and believe that female persons of the African-American Persuasion are third in the social order of acceptance, respect, and power (i.e., first-Caucasian males, second-Caucasian females, third-African-American females, and fourth-African-American males). Most Interviewees articulated that they worked hard to get where they are in the workforce to realize their American dream but believe African-American females lack the enthusiasm and tenacity to achieve the same. The interviewees believe that if female persons of the African-America Persuasion work hard, they can ascend to equivalent financially and educational designations. The interviewees further expound that Caucasians and African-American have had the same equal opportunities and equal playing fields to accomplish any goal. In multiple instances, the respondents voluntarily attempted to dispel any argument that they historically participated in measures that lawfully thwarted African-American females any financial and educational progression that contributed to their present disparities. Below are some of the Caucasian females' further potent dissection and preconceptions of female persons of the African-American Persuasion.

They don't work well with each other.
They don't shop in their community.
They don't appreciate or accept their beauty.
They don't aim high but settle for mediocrity.
They don't require (with the absence of being
cantankerous) respect from others.
They don't have regular or annual health screenings.
They don't lift each other.
They place heavy emphases on hair, nails,
jewelry, clothes, and shoe.
They heavily support other ethnic business, but not their own.
They are aggressive and impenitent drivers.
They incite verbal and physical altercations
of themselves and others.

They wear cumbersome and excessive accessories.
They wear tight clothing for most occasions
some of which may not be appropriate.
They are quick to use invective (swear) language.
They are quick to be agitated and cause harm to others.
They are resilient and expressively strong.
They adapt to any challenge they face.
They reveal in the notion that they prefer being independent.
They often wear extremely long wigs or
weave hair, nails, and eyelashes.
They (millennials) are quick to call each other
demeaning names as "bitches, tricks, and hoes."
They are quick to argue and argue loudly.
They are naturally beautiful.
They are very creative and smart.
They exaggeratedly accentuate their curvature figures.
They frequently eat unhealthy foods and
introduce their families to the same.
They frequently speak ill and negative of each other.
They are stressed more often than others.
They usually have to pamper themselves.
They are frequently upset with their child or children's father (s).
They have natural curvy and attractive figures.

Why is it that most female interviewees of the African-American Persuasion expressed that they have observed and believe that most female persons of the Caucasian Persuasion are commonly accepted as victims in every facet of society? Most of the interviewees believe that a significant number of Caucasian females are privileged and display acute arrogance of said observation. The majority of interviewees hesitantly articulated that they had experienced frequent and varied instances where they were ignored, shunned, and looked over or denied by Caucasian females because of their ethnicity when they were vying for employment, academic advancement, commercial advertisement, modeling, and other opportunities. They believe most Caucasian females are informed at an early age to project a physical and emotional fragile temperament to manipulate most of the society to favor their interest. Most Interviewees continued to articulate that they believe most Caucasian females are given extraordinary opportunities to advance in most businesses with little education, experience, and longevity than them. The interviewees amplified the notion that the Caucasian female historically and willfully participated in actions that lawfully thwarted African-American females and males significant financial and educational progression that contributed to their present disparities. Below are some of the African-American females' additional potent characterizations and preconceptions of female persons of the Caucasian Persuasion.

They don't socialize with other ethnic groups.
They don't shop in other ethnic groups' communities.
They don't appreciate or accept another ethnic groups' beauty.
They don't aim high but settle for mediocrity.
They blindly expect respect from others.
They have regular or annual health screenings.
They project a sense of innocent but will
disparage others at the drop of a hat.
They expose their children to cultural events
and active in their children's education.

They are professionals at stealing, cheating,
lying, spending another peoples' money.
They place moderate emphases on hair,
nails, jewelry, clothes, and shoe.
They heavily support each other's businesses
and enjoy evenings out with each other.
They are patient drivers.
They have a propensity to seem fragile when guilty of
wrong doings that cause others to defend them.
They dress in bland clothing and light accessories.
They dress in simple and loose clothing for most occasions.
They are quick to blame others.
They have an inclination to manipulate
others to do misdeeds for them.
They are lazy and expect others to do their
work but demand the credit.
They are not very good at adapting to financial challenges.
They expect everyone to take care of them.
They loathe the concept of being independent.
They choose not to accept the aging process.
They fixate over the need to have their
breast enhanced or enlarged.
They accept verbal and physical abuse from their
spouse more often particularly if he is wealthy.
They are quick to remarry.
They have been taught that they are the most
beautiful women in the world.
They are vindictive but usually get others to do their dirty work.
They have been taught that everything that is right
about other ethnic groups is not good for them
They are easily stressed and heavy prescription drug users.

23.2.4.13